THE OFFICIAL FANS' GUIDE 1997

TM

THIS IS A CARLTON BOOK

This edition published in 1997

10 9 8 7 6 5 4 3 2 1

A CIP catalogue record for this book is available from the British Library

Paperback ISBN 1 85868 257 6
Hardback ISBN 1 85868 318 1

Project editor: Martin Corteel
Project art direction: Paul Messam
Production: Garry Lewis
Picture research: Lorna Ainger
Designed by Nigel Davies

Author's acknowledgements

My special thanks to Joanne Lumley at *Open Rugby* Magazine for all her help
with the producing of this book. I would also like to thank David Ballheimer,
Raymond Fletcher, John Bailie and Tom Easton for their assistance with the
text and Andrew Varley, Jay Town, Trevor McKewen and the Stills Department
at Sky Television for their advice with the sourcing of the photographs.

THE OFFICIAL FANS' GUIDE 1997

™

HARRY EDGAR

CARLTON

CONTENTS

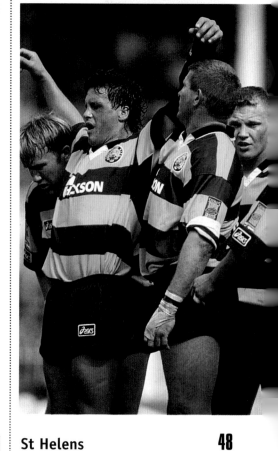

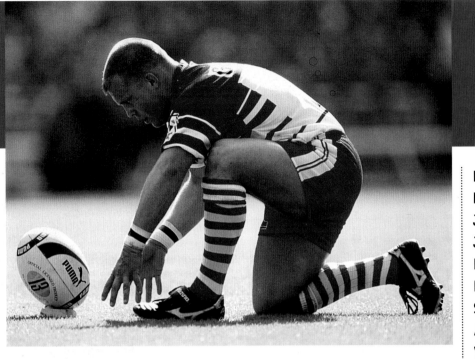

Opposite: top left: Stones Super League trophy; bottom left: Keiron Cunningham (left) of St Helens; top right: Castleford pack waiting for a scrum; This page: top: Bobbie Goulding, lining up a kick; left: Andrew Ettingshausen, Australian superstar

INTRODUCTION

by Mike "Stevo" Stephenson

We saw last year just what an impact Stones Super League can have on the game. The switch to summer was a big success, and on the firm grounds the game was faster and more exciting than ever.

On Sky Sports we covered the Stones Super League season from the very first kick in Paris to the very last tackle at Old Trafford, and I can't remember a single mediocre game all year. It was rip-roaring action all the way.

The introduction of the video referee in the televised games also brought a new dimension to the entertainment. Certainly we in the commentary box were holding our breath just as tightly as the fans as we awaited crucial decisions to be made. And there were plenty of times when the use of our new technology made vital decisions that, in the past, would have put enormous pressure on the referees.

The camera does not lie, and Stones Super League has pioneered the way ahead for all sports.

1997 is going to be even better. With a year's experience behind them, all the clubs will be much better prepared and ready to attract even bigger crowds and put on even more spectacular entertainment.

After a long winter break the fans will be hungry for Rugby League, and the summer conditions will ensure that the vast array of superstars in the game can put all their skills on show.

The game can't look back. The idea of big-city clubs like London and Paris and teams playing in super stadiums has to be the way ahead.

And now we can welcome the teams from down-under into the Stones Super League World Club Championship, it's going to be sensational.

It won't be easy for our British clubs, but the prospect of seeing such teams as the Canberra Raiders, Brisbane Broncos and Auckland Warriors over here is mouth-watering for the fans. And I know all the Stones Super League coaches are looking forward to the challenge in a big way.

Saints broke Wigan's dominance of the game last season, and in 1997 there will be no shortage of determined challengers.

I can't wait for the 1997 season – and we'll be following it in detail all the way on Sky Sports. All the crucial moments – every try, every goal, every hit … we'll be there.

I'm sure this Official Fans' Guide will help your enjoyment of Stones Super League in 1997. With features on all the clubs, the Australasian clubs and the leading superstars of the game, it's the perfect companion to Stones Super League for fans, new and old. And I'll bet we'll be seeing an awful lot of new fans in '97 as Stones Super League really takes off.

Happy reading … and happy viewing.

Stevo!

MIKE STEPHENSON,
former Great Britain international,
now Sky Sports' resident Rugby League expert

ORIGINS OF SUPER LEAGUE

Same game, different attitude!

In 1986, Wigan director Jack Robinson gave a prophetic interview at the invitation of Open Rugby magazine. He claimed: "We need a Super League and we need it now!" Jack felt that the British game would go nowhere fast if it continued to restrict itself to small-town clubs existing on tradition alone, happy to be biggish fish in a small pond, rather than striving to expand and develop the game to the kind of potential it deserved.

PARTNERS ... Britain's Maurice Lindsay with New Zealand's Graham Carden

Nine years later British Rugby League was in its one hundredth year and looking forward to centenary celebrations when, one morning in April 1995, a bombshell hit the game. It emerged from an extraordinary meeting of Rugby League Council members held at Wigan's Central Park that decisions had been taken that would change the face of the game forever.

The League's chief executive, Maurice Lindsay, announced that the British game had accepted an £87 million five-year television contract proposal from Rupert Murdoch's News Limited. The Council had also agreed to make the revolutionary switch to a summer season to enable it to run in tandem with the new Super League Murdoch's company was attempting to set up in Australia.

They also originally agreed that numerous British clubs would pool resources and create new merged teams representing wider areas of population. However, the last suggestion prompted such vitriolic and emotional reaction from the supporters of those clubs who were scheduled to disappear into mergers that,

THE GRAND OPENING ... Fireworks greet the arrival of Paris Saint Germain as Super League kicks off at Charlety Stadium

within a month, the League had back-tracked and announced that the new Stones Super League would go ahead with a three-divisional structure including all the existing clubs.

The new format would see the majority of resources put into the elite level of the game – the Stones Super League, with the promise from BSkyB television that it would be promoted as never before.

"Same game, different attitude" was the motto adopted by Stones Super League officials as the switch to a summer season was confirmed and the whole face of the game was set to be changed.

Stones Super League talked of its world vision to take the game around the globe via Rupert Murdoch's television empire. Fans and players alike were excited by the prospects of expanded international competition – including the World Nines, the Oceania Cup and, most crucial of all, the World Club Championship play-offs between the top teams in both European and Australasian Super Leagues.

The excitement, however, had to be tempered for a while with the knowledge that in Australia Super League, originally had been born out of a battle for Pay Television rights and, unless Rupert Murdoch's company's plans were given the green light by the law courts Down Under, the European end of the operation might not be able to take advantage of the exciting opportunities. The vision would remain just a dream – whilst it all depended on the lawyers and judges to make it happen.

SHAPING THE FUTURE

Innovations that were to come with Stones Super League were the inclusion of a Paris team, taking the first steps towards a European competition, and several new rules aimed at speeding up and streamlining the game on the field even more. These included the non-scoring side receiving the kick-off following a score, and a tackled player no longer being allowed to get up and play-the-ball to himself.

A highlight of the new Stones Super League was the installation of the so-called "video referee", in which at BSkyB televised games a fourth official used the video replays to rule on unclear try-scoring decisions when requested to do so by the match referee. This practical use of the available technology was a great help to referees to ensure they got the correct rulings, and the tense wait for the decision to be flashed up on the big screen added considerable drama to Stones Super League games for spectators.

These were some of the things that were to give Stones Super League its new face. They were all part of the philosophy "to promote Rugby League like it's never been seen before."

START OF THE DREAM ... Wigan's Gary Connolly in the 1994 World Club Challenge match against Brisbane Broncos at ANZ Stadium

Super League World Club Championship

It was a balmy night in Brisbane as two of the super powers of Rugby League went head-to-head in a battle for the self-styled World Club Challenge.

On that night, 1 June, 1994, Wigan beat the Broncos to strike a blow for British credibility after years of disappointment in the international arena against the Aussies. More importantly, as rival officials like John Ribot, Barry Maranta, Maurice Lindsay and Jack

Robinson surveyed the huge crowd at ANZ Stadium and enjoyed the spectacle of Rugby League on the big stage, the seeds of an idea were firmly planted.

It may have been just a dream at the time – a vision of what might be. But the idea of big-city teams across the world contesting a global competition was a mouth-watering prospect when those officials considered the potential television audiences and commercial opportunities that would be generated to help promote the game as never before.

Throughout the near-century of its eventful life Rugby League had struggled to break out of its traditional heartland and to attract the wider audience it surely deserved. Would the impetus of having high-profile clubs, serving big cities and whole areas of population on the same lines as the National Football League in America, put Rugby League on a higher level than anything it had known before? Apart from the struggling London team – almost 15 years old and still distinctly minor league, with crowds of just over 700 – Rugby League's attempts at expansion outside its Yorkshire-Lancashire-Cheshire-Cumbria heartland had met with complete failure.

So, as Messrs Lindsay, Robinson and the triumphant Wigan team flew home to the north of England, the dream remained just that – a dream. Nobody in Britain had taken much notice of Robinson's ideas in *Open Rugby* back in 1986. Rugby League was being given greater coverage on BSkyB television under the banner of "The Big League", but the clubs remained essentially small-time.

Broncos buck the system

But for John Ribot and his Brisbane Broncos, something more was stirring the night they entertained Wigan in 1994. There was a frustration, even anger, brewing at the Broncos. They were unhappy with many things about the Australian Rugby League (still known at that time as the New South Wales Rugby

LEADER OF THE PACK ... John Ribot, Super League's front man in the battle with the A.R.L.

League). Sure, the Broncos played in their competition and were grateful to have been first given the opportunity in 1988, but Brisbane felt that in many ways they had now outgrown the League.

The Broncos were a hugely successful commercial organization. They had the whole of corporate Brisbane, and most of Queensland, queuing up to be involved as sponsors, and their merchandising operation was mega. And since they weathered the storm of criticism as they moved out of Lang Park and into ANZ Stadium, they had drawn crowds of over 50,000 to games whilst some other teams in the same competition were struggling to get 3,000–4,000 to home matches.

It was a lopsided competition and everybody in Australia knew it. However, far from the League looking to take on board more of the expertise that had made Brisbane so successful by giving them a greater say in the destiny of the game, just the opposite was happening.

Broncos officials, especially Ribot, quite clearly were given the impression that they had become too big for their boots. The rivalry between a NSW-based and administered competition and the "interlopers" from Queensland hardly helped. The Sydney-based power brokers claimed the Brisbane boys had a major chip on their shoulders, finding an ulterior motive for every decision that went against them in their paranoia that everybody else in the game was determined to bring them down a peg or two. Whether the Broncos' beliefs were real or imagined, it was glaringly obvious that a split was brewing.

Different country, same problems

Most people in Australian League acknowledged that there was some need for a rationalization of their competition – that there were too many teams in Sydney and that there was no way some traditional old clubs in suburbs with diminishing or changing populations could ever hope to compete commercially with the giant one-city outfits like

CAPITAL AWAKENING ... Large crowds were attracted to watch the London Broncos at The Valley in Super League

Brisbane, Canberra, Auckland, Newcastle or Townsville (North Queensland Cowboys' home).

But the changes steadfastly refused to come. Call it loyalty to fine traditions or call it the old pals' act, the truth was, despite all its success in expansion nationwide, increasing overall crowds and sponsorship, and the impact of the pioneering Tina Turner commercials, League in Australia was ripe for change. It was a victim of its own success.

That's where Rupert Murdoch's News Limited came into the ball-park. Pay TV was on its way into Australia and nobody knew better than Mr Murdoch that to make Pay TV succeed you had to have the leading sport on your channel. He'd proved it quite conclusively both in England, by tying up Premier League soccer for Sky, and in America, by securing the NFL for Fox. And in Australia, where by far the largest chunk of the population is centred around Sydney, there is only one sport that counts when it comes to attracting top TV ratings – Rugby League.

News Limited approached the Australian Rugby League with a plan to restructure the competition and get themselves a slice of the television pie. But the ARL – already contracted to Mr Murdoch's arch-rival media mogul Kerry Packer – wouldn't, or couldn't, play ball.

War of the moguls

News Limited had to get Rugby League for their Pay TV channel – and, without the co-operation of the ARL, the only way they could achieve that was by setting up their own Rugby League competition to put on their screens. And so began the bitter "war" between Super League and the ARL, one that was to occupy the time of a host of the top legal eagles and fill vast acres of newsprint for over a year.

That's where the British game came in as part of the big picture as Super League's "vision" of worldwide promotion of the game, via Mr Murdoch's television empire, was cast in stone.

The Australian Rugby League's trump card in their attempts to rebuff Super League was the promise of international competition. The lure of the green and gold jumper was still a massive incentive for all Aussie players. But Super League trumped the trump by taking the opposition away at a stroke. Both the British and New Zealand Leagues signed up with Super League, and a dagger was plunged into the heart of the ARL.

Summer football

The world vision of Stones Super League enabled the game in Britain to fulfil its ambitions to switch to a summer season to run alongside the southern hemisphere. The introduction of Paris, and greater emphasis put on London – now owned by Brisbane shareholder Barry Maranta and re-nicknamed the Broncos – both "fast-tracked" into Super League for 1996, also coincided neatly with News Limited's plan to take the game to a bigger, more cosmopolitan audience.

The financial input from News Limited to the British game came as something of a lifeline for the clubs and enabled the Super League teams to make their players full-time professionals. There was also an emphasis on improving stadium facilities and putting on a show like never before to make Rugby League a spectacle of family entertainment.

A new catchphrase came into use in the British game, that it should be "marketing-led". Clubs were encouraged to invest in packages of pre-match and half-time entertainment, bringing singers, rock bands and dancing girls into the arenas to attract younger audiences and greater numbers of females to the game.

Furthermore minimum standards were instituted so that clubs were in no doubt as to the quality of the stadiums they were required to inhabit in this brave new world. For some clubs, however, it would take millions of pounds to put right the neglect which their grounds had suffered for decades.

The British game desperately needed the impetus and financial support that

KEEPING COOL ... Summer Rugby and Super League came to Castleford

the new television contract brought, whilst the switch to summer presented major new opportunities. As the Stones Super League in Europe got under way in 1996, however, the whole master plan for a global championship was put on hold after the Australian Super League was rebuffed in the Australian courts.

The first appeal followed the decision of the original court and in 1996 the European Super League went it alone. But, when a spectacularly successful second appeal gave Australian Super League the go-ahead in early October 1996, the world vision was given the green light.

The 1997 World Club Championship games will provide a new focal point for the British clubs and their fans, and with the next World Cup scheduled for Australia in 1998 – just two years before the Sydney Olympics – a new spirit of internationalism is present in the world of Rugby League.

That world vision has to be the key to Super League's success. It can transport the game on to a higher plane. The vision has been present among some followers of Rugby League for a very long time – but now Super League, with television around the world playing an essential role, has the opportunity to make the dreams become reality.

REVIEW OF THE 1996 SEASON

One Giant Step ...

Rugby League held its breath as the inaugural season of Super League approached. After so much controversy and confusion, just how would the game, its players and, most importantly, its public adapt to the big switch to a summer season? And how would the clubs rise to the challenges put before them in adopting the Super League philosophy of providing big entertainment on a big stage?

The British game had wrapped up its Centenary season at the end of January 1996, and had just a two-month break before the great adventure was scheduled to kick off in Paris. Super League's search for a European identity had led to the creation of the Paris Saint Germain team, immediately giving the code the major publicity boost of carrying the label of one of Europe's most famous football clubs.

And another capital city team, the London Broncos, were primed to give Super League a double-pronged

promotional boost on either side of the Channel. The Broncos were seen by many as the unknown quantity before the 1996 Super League season started. But, with an influx of new Australian players, largely with better-quality track records than most who had gone before, the suspicion was that they might hold, if not a few aces, then at least a couple of wild-cards. As events turned out, the Broncos were actually holding the Super League joker up their sleeves when Terry Matterson kicked a touchline conversion to clinch an 18-all draw at Wigan in mid-season.

Once people had put aside any doubts on the switch to summer, or the other significant changes taking place in the game, the one burning question waiting to be answered in the 1996 season – as it had been in the previous five or six seasons – was, could anybody overhaul Wigan? Popular assumption was that this year, bearing in mind that Wigan had lost several experienced and established star players, somebody could – and that somebody was most likely to be their arch local rivals St Helens!

Saints had a new coach in Shaun McRae, a man with vast experience with both the Canberra Raiders and Kangaroo touring teams, and they had the world's most expensive player in Paul Newlove ready to prove just why he was worth over half a million pounds to the Saints.

Other popular predictions were that the Bradford Bulls would enjoy the same kind of leap in standards seen at all the other clubs their charismatic coach Brian Smith had taken charge of, and that

CAPITAL CITY POWER ... The London Broncos gave Super League a double-pronged promotional boost on both sides of the Channel

CONTRASTING IMAGES ... Jules Parry leads a Paris charge at Workington – two sides from the opposite extremes of Super League

Leeds would continue to be just one step behind favourites Wigan and St Helens. Only one of those hot tips proved to be inaccurate.

Workington Town, without the big financial or sponsorship base of other clubs in higher population centres, knew they were going to struggle to survive in Super League – but less obvious were answers to the questions on how the middle-ground teams like Warrington, Castleford, Halifax or Oldham would fare. Would they be able to challenge the big guns for a play-off place and promote themselves in the manner envisaged by the new Super League?

So many questions were waiting to be answered as Super League began its first great summer adventure in 1996. Five months of non-stop, action-packed football were to follow as the drama unfolded. The ultimate target was to be crowned the inaugural European Super League champions, but for the game as a whole the challenges were much more complex as it took one giant step into the future.

APRIL Super kick-off in Paris

Everything Super League hoped it could be was encapsulated in its grand opening night in Paris. The first season of Super League was to bring much drama and many great contests, but nothing could equal the sheer emotional theatre of its very first match when Paris put the 'Euro' into European Super League and kicked off the game's new era under floodlights at the magnificent state-of-the-art Charlety Stadium.

It turned into a dream come true for everybody except Paris's opponents, the Sheffield Eagles. A sensational crowd of almost 18,000 – reported as the biggest for a Rugby League match in France for 38 years – enjoyed the music, the fireworks and then the rip-roaring action and skills of Rugby League as Paris Saint Germain played like men inspired to storm to an opening victory by 30 points to 24.

The vision of big city clubs playing across Europe suddenly seemed as if it could become a reality. More so when, in Round Two, the 'Tale of Two Cities' crossed the Channel to London where a crowd of approaching 10,000 were attracted on a Thursday night to the Valley to see the Broncos' Super League home debut against Paris. The two capital city teams produced an 11-try feast of attacking Rugby League, and the new face of Super League was up and running with a bang.

Saints' ominous warning

But, while the national headlines were being dominated by London and Paris, back down at the nitty gritty, St Helens well and truly laid down the gauntlet to Wigan, the side who had dominated the Championship for the previous seven seasons.

Saints, with new coach Shaun McRae at the helm, hammered Workington at Derwent Park 62–0 in the opening round, and backed that up with another thrashing of Leeds at Headingley in Round Three. In between, St Helens gained the scalp they craved most of all, and sent shock waves throughout the game when they walloped Wigan 42–26 at Knowsley Road on Good Friday.

Saints' stunning attacking play, with teenage winger Danny Arnold rattling up nine touchdowns in the first three games, had torn apart the toughest defensive unit in the League. And in their new recruit from Australia, former Balmain forward Derek McVey, St Helens seemed to have found their Championship catalyst.

A Wembley break

The first month of Super League ended after five rounds with, to nobody's surprise, St Helens and Wigan leading the way. Both Halifax and Workington Town were left pointless as the League took a break to enjoy St Helens and the Bradford Bulls put on a Wembley spectacular in the Challenge Cup Final. Saints won that one 40–32, but the Bulls phenomenon was only just starting to click into gear.

Leeds finally got off the mark with a win in Round Five, but lost debut-making New Zealander Nathan Picci with a serious shoulder injury which ended his Headingley season after less than an hour on the pitch.

OPENING NIGHT ... Dean Lawford attacks at Charlety, but Paris were not to be denied as Super League kicked off

RESULTS

ROUND 1
29, 30 and 31 March

Bradford	30	18	Castleford
Halifax	22	24	London
Leeds	18	22	Warrington
Oldham	16	56	Wigan
Paris S.G.	30	24	Sheffield
Workington	0	62	St Helens

ROUND 2
4 and 5 April

Castleford	26	23	Leeds
London	38	22	Paris S.G.
Oldham	34	22	Halifax
Sheffield	40	24	Bradford
St Helens	41	26	Wigan
Warrington	45	30	Workington

ROUND 3
8 and 9 April

Bradford	31	24	London
Halifax	30	34	Castleford
Leeds	24	46	St Helens
Paris S.G.	24	24	Oldham
Wigan	42	12	Warrington
Workington	22	54	Sheffield

ROUND 4
12, 13 and 14 April

Castleford	10	28	Wigan
Oldham	25	16	Leeds
Paris S.G.	34	12	Bradford
St Helens	26	20	Bradford
Sheffield	34	18	London
Warrington	16	10	Halifax

ROUND 5
19, 20 and 21 April

Castleford	20	24	Oldham
Halifax	28	30	St Helens
Leeds	36	22	Sheffield
London	58	0	Workington
Warrington	48	24	Paris S.G.
Wigan	22	6	Bradford

SEISMIC INCIDENT

THE FRENCH FLIER!

Super League's opening night in Paris will live forever in the memories of those who saw it unfold before their very eyes. Emotions ran high all night, but they finally exploded when Paris St Germain winger Arnaud Cervello took a late interception and sprinted 80 yards down the left touchline to score with every one of the Charlety Stadium's 18,000 spectators on their feet – some in disbelief, others in ecstasy. It clinched a victory over the Sheffield Eagles that nobody really expected the new Paris team to achieve, and came after a thriller in which the lead frequently changed hands. The relief of Cervello's try was like a champagne cork popping – and copious amounts of the bubbly stuff flowed as a result on that famous night in Paris.

SUPER LEAGUE STANDINGS (at April 21, 1996)

	P	W	D	L	F	A	Pts
St Helens	5	5	0	0	205	98	10
Wigan	5	4	0	1	174	85	8
Warrington	5	4	0	1	143	124	8
Oldham Bears	5	3	1	1	123	138	7
London Broncos	5	3	0	2	162	109	6
Sheffield Eagles	5	3	0	2	174	130	6
Paris St Germain	5	2	1	2	134	146	5
Bradford Bulls	5	2	0	3	111	130	4
Castleford Tigers	5	2	0	3	108	135	4
Leeds	5	1	0	4	117	141	2
Halifax Blue Sox	5	0	0	5	112	138	0
Workington	5	0	0	5	64	253	0

MAY Saints set the trends

After the euphoria and initial uncertainties in the opening month of the European Super League, May got down to the business of seeing several trends start to emerge that were to shape the whole season.

Number one among those was the uncanny ability of St Helens to snatch victory from the jaws of defeat. Saints came into May on the back of their Challenge Cup Final victory at Wembley, and whilst they proceeded to run up cricket scores at home against Oldham and Castleford, they found London a much tougher nut to crack when the Broncos came north to Knowsley Road in Round Seven.

The Broncos had a commanding 22–8 lead over Saints before Bobbie Goulding's men hit back to scrape a 24–22 win. It was the start of an ongoing rivalry between St Helens and London, which

was to feature more hard-fought games, controversial moments and tough talking from their respective Australian coaches Shaun McRae and Tony Currie.

St Helens emerged at the end of May as the only undefeated team in Super League, but if they thought that Broncos' win was too close for comfort their fans' nerves were almost shattered a week later in an absolute thriller at Warrington. Saints did it by the skin of their teeth again. A 76th-minute try by rampaging front-rower Ian Pickavance got them home 25–24 after Warrington did everything but win the game on the scoreboard.

Saints must have known by then that 1996 was going to be a special season for them, and another giant was truly starting to stir at the vast Odsal Stadium as the Bulls emerged from their Wembley disappointment to go through May undefeated.

Bradford were starting to see a team of genuine quality emerge as individuals like Robbie Paul, Graeme Bradley, James Lowes and Steve McNamara began to knit together.

Wigan in Rugby Union

May was the month when Wigan took time out from Super League to dabble in the world of Rugby Union. Their historic cross-code challenges with 15-a-side champions Bath and victory in the Middlesex Sevens at Twickenham should have provided Rugby League with a wealth of highly positive publicity as they so clearly illustrated the superior athleticism, skills and entertainment value of League players. But, instead of provoking more widespread interest in Super League, this only appeared to spark a rush from the leading Rugby Union clubs to sign up the stars from League, most notably Wigan's own Jason Robinson and Henry Paul who were to head off to Bath.

CLASH OF THE CODES ... Henry Paul leads this Bath opponent a merry dance at Maine Road, where Wigan strolled to an 82–6 win

After their promising opening month the harsh realities of professional League started to hit home for Paris Saint Germain. With most of their players forced to double up and play for their local clubs in the domestic French Championship as well as for P.S.G., it was inevitable that fatigue, along with injuries, would take their toll.

Leeds cruise in Paris

It became the norm for each Paris away game in England to result in a heavy defeat. On home soil they had remained unbeaten in the first month, but in their first home game in May, Leeds, a side struggling to find any kind of form themselves, easily became the first visiting team to win at Charlety.

SEISMIC INCIDENT

A TRIP TOO FAR

Many people thought Wigan would be vulnerable when they travelled midweek to play improving Halifax at Thrum Hall in Round Seven after their frolics against Rugby Union opposition. Surely, their minds had been off the real job and their bodies relaxed at the drop in intensity?

But when Blue Sox forward Michael Jackson was sent off for an alleged trip in only the ninth minute any theories about a Wigan weakness were thrown out the window as the game was handed to them on a plate. It was later shown that Jackson's was a clear case of mistaken identity – an error that proved so generous for Wigan.

WEMBLEY WIZARDS ... Saints with the Challenge Cup

Another magnificent crowd, 15,107, provided a sensational atmosphere among the music and fireworks of Paris but, with several key P.S.G. men playing just 48 hours after giving their all in the French Championship semi-finals, the Loiners cruised to a 40–14 victory inspired by Kevin Iro looking awesome in one of his increasingly rare unstoppable performances.

May was Workington Town's best month, a draw at home to Halifax and a win at Oldham bringing three points and a glimmer of hope which was to burn out almost as quickly as it appeared. The Blue Sox themselves finally turned promise into points, as victories began to come and start the climb back to the top half of the table for Steve Simms' team.

RESULTS

ROUND 6
3, 5 and 6 May

Bradford	36	14	Warrington
Leeds	20	27	London
Sheffield	20	12	Castleford
St Helens	66	18	Oldham
Wigan	76	8	Paris S.G.
Workington	18	18	Halifax

ROUND 7
10 and 12 May

Halifax	4	50	Wigan
Oldham	10	30	Bradford
Castleford	50	16	Workington
St Helens	24	22	London
Paris S.G.	14	40	Leeds
Warrington	36	26	Sheffield

ROUND 8
17, 18 and 19 May

Bradford	60	32	Paris S.G.
Castleford	20	21	London
Leeds	18	32	Halifax
Sheffield	23	10	Oldham
Warrington	24	25	St Helens
Workington	16	64	Wigan

ROUND 9
24, 25, 26 and 27 May

Bradford	54	8	Leeds
Oldham	26	29	Workington
Paris S.G.	10	38	Halifax
St Helens	62	24	Castleford
Warrington	28	24	London
Wigan	50	6	Sheffield

SUPER LEAGUE STANDINGS (at May 27, 1996)

	P	W	D	L	F	A	Pts
St Helens	9	9	0	0	382	186	18
Wigan	9	8	0	1	414	119	16
Bradford Bulls	9	6	0	3	291	194	12
Warrington	9	6	0	3	245	235	12
London Broncos	9	5	0	4	256	201	10
Sheffield Eagles	9	5	0	4	249	238	10
Oldham Bears	9	3	1	5	188	286	7
Castleford Tigers	9	3	0	6	214	254	6
Halifax Blue Sox	9	2	1	6	204	234	5
Paris St Germain	9	2	1	6	198	360	5
Leeds	9	2	0	7	203	268	4
Workington	9	1	1	7	143	412	3

JUNE

The significant improvement in the London Broncos proved to be a major achievement of the 1996 Super League season. Coach Tony Currie turned the Broncos into very tough opponents, often awkward to play against and with a steely defence building the platform for numerous top performances against the high flyers of the League.

Currie had long ringed the date of 9 June on his fixture calendar. A visit to Central Park in Round 11 to meet Wigan was seen as the acid test for the travelling Australians – and they exceeded even their coach's expectations against the side which had dominated the British game for so many years.

The Broncos frustrated both the Wigan team and the Central Park crowd, forcing Graeme West's boys on to the back foot and into uncharacteristic errors. And that crowd, who had spent much of the afternoon booing, were stunned into silence when Broncos' skipper Terry Matterson dramatically converted a late try from the touchline to tie the scores at 18–all.

Currie and the Broncos were delirious, Wigan were grumpy and their arch rivals, St Helens, celebrated the dropped point that was to prove oh so vital in the race for the title.

Saints, however, suffered the backlash from wounded Wigan two weeks later when Central Park housed Super League's biggest attendance of the season and the visitors tasted their first defeat of the season after 12 straight wins.

International flavour

Whilst Wigan and St Helens jousted for the role as top dog throughout June, it was also the month when Super League's European International Championship was staged. The event appeared fairly low-key, with the Welsh team severely weakened after their inspirational shows in the Centenary World Cup, and France desperately tired, dispirited and out of their depth.

England merely did what they had to

UNSTOPPABLE ... Va'aiga Tuigamala was in awesome form as Wigan ended the Saints' 100 per cent record

do, outclassing France 73–6 at Gateshead and then clinching the championship, under the captaincy of Andy Farrell, by beating Wales 26–12 at Cardiff Arms Park. The Welsh had earlier triumphed 34–14 over France at Carcassonne.

The conclusion of the European Championship at least had a positive effect on the Paris Saint Germain side who had become exhausted, mentally and physically, by having most of their players back up for their local clubs as well as playing for Paris in Super League. The end of the French domestic season was immediately followed by the European Championship, so still there was no respite for the beleaguered Frenchmen.

Their nightmare came to a head when, just 48 hours after most of their team had played for France against Wales, Castleford visited the Charlety Stadium in stifling heat and romped in for 54 points. Things couldn't get any worse for Paris, and they finally got to enjoy the luxury of their players only having one game a week to concentrate on by the time Round 13 arrived at the end of June. The upsurge in their performance was as dramatic as it was immediate, as P.S.G. were desperately unlucky to lose 26–24 to Warrington.

Tigers maul the Bulls

Castleford, fresh from their points-fest in Paris, came home to claim one of the biggest scalps of the season when they turned over Bradford in the Yorkshire derby in Round 12. It was a hiccup for the Bulls, emerging as a growing force in Super League, which was set to show its full potential in July.

Broncos' vital point

SEISMIC INCIDENT

RESULTS

ROUND 10
31 May, 1 and 2 June

Bradford	52	4	Workington
Castleford	17	22	Warrington
Halifax	33	30	Sheffield
Leeds	20	40	Wigan
London	28	22	Oldham
St Helens	52	10	Paris S.G.

ROUND 11
7, 8 and 9 June

Halifax	20	22	Bradford
Oldham	35	24	Warrington
Paris S.G.	22	54	Castleford
Sheffield	32	43	St Helens
Wigan	18	18	London
Workington	18	48	Leeds

ROUND 12
14, 15 and 16 June

Castleford	26	23	Bradford
London	24	52	Halifax
Sheffield	52	18	Paris S.G.
St Helens	60	16	Workington
Warrington	36	12	Leeds
Wigan	44	16	Oldham

ROUND 13
21, 22 and 23 June

Bradford	64	22	Sheffield
Halifax	14	20	Oldham
Leeds	25	18	Castleford
Paris S.G.	24	26	Warrington
Wigan	35	19	St Helens
Workington	6	34	London

ROUND 14
28, 29 and 30 June

Castleford	20	24	Halifax
London	16	22	Bradford
Oldham	24	6	Paris S.G.
St Helens	42	16	Leeds
Sheffield	32	16	Workington
Warrington	0	21	Wigan

TERRY'S DREAM KICK

Toe-poke goal-kickers are a rarity now in Rugby League, a nostalgic treat from bygone years. But London captain Terry Matterson has no reason to change from the old style. His touchline conversion in the dying moments of the Broncos' Round 11 thriller at Wigan stunned the Central Park crowd. It didn't just earn London an 18–18 draw, more importantly, it took away the point from Wigan that was, eventually, to deny the cherry and whites the Super League title. Few goal-kicks have been as vital.

SUPER LEAGUE STANDINGS (at June 30, 1996)

	P	W	D	L	F	A	Pts
St Helens	14	13	0	1	598	295	26
Wigan	14	12	1	1	572	192	25
Bradford Bulls	14	10	0	4	474	282	20
Warrington	14	9	0	5	353	344	18
London Broncos	14	7	1	6	376	321	15
Sheffield Eagles	14	7	0	7	417	412	14
Oldham Bears	14	6	1	7	305	402	13
Halifax Blue Sox	14	5	1	8	347	350	11
Castleford Tigers	14	5	0	9	349	370	10
Leeds	14	4	0	10	324	422	8
Paris St Germain	14	2	1	11	278	568	5
Workington	14	1	1	12	203	638	3

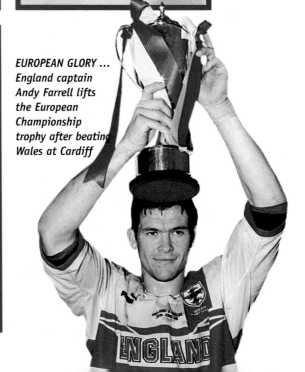

EUROPEAN GLORY ... England captain Andy Farrell lifts the European Championship trophy after beating Wales at Cardiff

JULY The Bulls stampede

ALL SPRUCED UP ... Bradford Bulls full-back Stuart Spruce was in brilliant form as Wigan were beaten on a memorable night at Odsal Stadium in July

Top two hanging on

Bradford's memorable victories over both title contenders, St Helens and Wigan, followed by a rip-roaring win in a battle at Warrington, confirmed them as Super League's outstanding team in July. But while the Bulls were stampeding all before them, Saints and Wigan were hanging on to the top two positions by the skin of their teeth – and both had controversial refereeing decisions to thank.

Wigan needed an injury-time penalty by Andy Farrell to beat Castleford 26–25, after former Central Park hero Frano Botica's late field-goal had put the Tigers one point ahead.

Then St Helens truly got out of jail against London when Apollo Perelini, on the say-so of the video referee, was awarded a late, late try that broke the Broncos' hearts after a sensational game at The Valley.

That ensured Saints were still at the top as the Super League season entered its final month, but July had seen the competition really come alive with those two epic nights at Odsal and the tension surrounding the leaders in such nail-biting encounters.

'Le Crunch' in Cumbria

Drama was also the name of the game at the bottom as Workington entertained Paris Saint Germain in Round 15 in a match they billed as 'Le Crunch'. The Cumbrians, anchored to the bottom all season, felt the whole world was against them in their belief that Paris were being given extra help to avoid relegation, and on an emotional night at Derwent Park Workington achieved their only home victory of the season.

That put Town level with Paris on five points each, but their new optimism about getting away from bottom spot lasted just six days as Paris turned round and beat London on Bastille Day to restore the two-point gap.

Paris, now with coaching guidance

Ever since the Wembley Challenge Cup Final the Bradford Bulls had been promising St Helens would get 'pay-back time' when they went to Odsal Stadium on 5 July. And the ambush plan worked to perfection as the Saints really didn't know what hit them when the Bulls ripped them apart in a stunning display of Rugby League skills, rattling up a half-century of points against the League leaders.

If that was an epic performance by Bradford, July was to bring even greater glories for Brian Smith's Bulls. Seven days after hammering St Helens, Bradford also rolled over Wigan in front of Odsal Stadium's biggest League match crowd for over 20 years – 17,360. And the Bulls did it with 12 men, pulling back a 10–0 deficit after second-rower Jeremy Donougher had been sent off. It was awesome stuff.

SEISMIC INCIDENT

APOLLO TOUCHDOWN!

Crunch decisions don't come any closer or more controversial than the one which saw Apollo Perelini awarded a try for St Helens in injury-time at the London Broncos in Round 18. Saints had been making a habit of getting out of jail, but this was the moment they knew, well and truly, that their name was written on the Super League trophy. As Apollo launched himself over a stacked Broncos defensive line, the last seconds were ticking away and St Helens were 28–26 down. It took an agonizingly long wait for the video referee to make one of his toughest decisions of the season.

from the RFL's John Kear, had improved to the point where they went on to scare the life out of Wigan in a 24–20 humdinger at the Charlety Stadium. But the Frenchmen could not repeat that form when they travelled for another crunch match against third from bottom Leeds. This was the game in which coach Dean Bell came out of retirement and scored a try to clinch victory for the Headingley team and ease all fears of relegation for Leeds.

RESULTS

ROUND 15
5, 6 and 7 July

Bradford	50	22	St Helens
Halifax	25	18	Warrington
Leeds	26	28	Oldham
London	45	8	Sheffield
Workington	14	10	Paris S.G.
Wigan	26	25	Castleford

ROUND 16
12, 13 and 14 July

Bradford	20	12	Wigan
Oldham	20	30	Castleford
Paris S.G.	24	18	London
Sheffield	34	31	Leeds
St Helens	58	20	Halifax
Workington	4	49	Warrington

ROUND 17
19, 20 and 21 July

Castleford	36	31	Sheffield
Halifax	74	14	Workington
London	33	16	Leeds
Oldham	18	54	St Helens
Paris S.G.	20	24	Wigan
Warrington	20	30	Bradford

ROUND 18
26, 27 and 28 July

Bradford	56	0	Oldham
Leeds	34	12	Paris S.G.
London	28	32	St Helens
Sheffield	28	22	Warrington
Wigan	34	26	Halifax
Workington	20	46	Castleford

SUPER LEAGUE STANDINGS (at July 28, 1996)

	P	W	D	L	F	A	Pts
St Helens	18	16	0	2	764	411	32
Wigan	18	15	1	2	668	283	31
Bradford Bulls	18	14	0	4	630	336	28
Warrington	18	10	0	8	462	431	20
London Broncos	18	9	1	8	500	401	19
Sheffield Eagles	18	9	0	9	518	546	18
Castleford Tigers	18	8	0	10	486	467	16
Halifax Blue Sox	18	7	1	10	492	474	15
Oldham Bears	18	7	1	10	371	568	15
Leeds	18	5	0	13	431	529	10
Paris St Germain	18	3	1	14	344	658	7
Workington	18	2	1	15	255	817	5

AUGUST *St Helens clinch title*

THE WINNERS ... St Helens celebrate the Super League title after beating Warrington

left on the clock at Castleford, McRae could see all his season's work crumbling before his very eyes as Tigers' full-back Jason Flowers broke clear and headed for the Saints' line. When his opposite number, Steve Prescott, appeared to make a try-saving tackle the sighs of relief could be heard all the way back across the East Lancs. Road to St Helens.

Celebrating in the rain

From then on it was plain sailing for Saints. A week later an army of their fans crossed the Channel to Paris and celebrated in the pouring rain among Charlety's smallest crowd of the season. Both Sheffield and Warrington were to prove no major obstacles for St Helens in subsequent weeks.

Meanwhile, Martin Offiah made his debut for London as the Broncos beat Warrington, a victory that was ultimately to give Tony Currie's team a play-off place ahead of the Wire. The Broncos then drew their biggest crowd of the season to the Valley in Round 21 when Wigan came to town.

And for almost an hour London looked to be handing the title on a plate to St Helens as they held the Riversiders at bay. But then on came Shaun Edwards from the interchange bench, and within two minutes he had scored the crucial try to put Wigan in front. By the time the final hooter came Wigan led by 21 points, with such as Tuigamala, Henry Paul and Jason Robinson still looking awesome – but they were rapidly running out of games.

Home town grit

Paris Saint Germain's significant improvement after John Kear took over the coaching reins was never more apparent than when they visited Kear's home town, Castleford, in Super League's penultimate round. Paris came agonizingly close to winning their first away game, despite playing the second half a man short after skipper Pierre Chamorin's dismissal.

MARTIN OFFIAH ... On his debut for the London Broncos against Warrington. His signing was a major coup for the Capital city team

The home run to the Super League title saw St Helens come into August on top of the table, still with their one-point advantage over Wigan. The Central Park outfit, with the bombshell prospect of losing their grip on the championship now actually dawning as a very serious reality, moved up a gear after midsummer hiccups and looked awesome throughout August.

Wigan were even confident enough in the ability of their young players to be able to unload Martin Offiah to the London Broncos. The transfer gave the Broncos their longed-for, high-profile London born star, and at the same time allowed the financially-pressed Wigan club more relief at the bank.

But Wigan knew no matter how well they played, and no matter how many points they rattled up, it would all be in vain if St Helens also won their remaining four games in August.

The Saints' toughest test came at Castleford in Round 19. Coach Shaun McRae realized that if his boys could tame the Tigers at Wheldon Road, the run-in to the title looked fairly smooth and unhindered. But, with only seconds

SEISMIC INCIDENT

FLOWERS PLUCKED

It was to be the last nail-biting escape for St Helens. Leading Castleford by just four points as the seconds ticked down on the clock at Wheldon Road in Round 19, Tigers' full-back Jason Flowers was clear and sprinting towards the St Helens line and looking a dead-cert try scorer. Saints fans and players were seeing their dream of the Super League title being plucked from their grasp with every yard of Flowers' run when, summoning an incredible surge of pace, Steve Prescott emerged from nowhere to cut him down short of the goal-line. It was a tackle that saved not just a try, even a game, but a whole season!

Moving the other way were Bradford, struck by the hammer blow of learning their inspirational coach Brian Smith was headed back to Australia to join the Parramatta club for 1997. This news coincided with a down-turn in the Bulls' performances, culminating in their first and only home defeat of the season when neighbours Halifax went to Odsal in Round 21 and won 27–26 thanks to a drop-goal by their captain, John Schuster.

And so the climax to the inaugural Super League championship came, as the scriptwriters had hoped, in the very last round. Wigan did everything in their power, hammering relegated Workington Town 78–4, but could only look on helplessly as St Helens cruised home 66–18 against Warrington. It left Bobbie Goulding to lift the trophy among joyous scenes before a capacity 18,000-crowd at Knowsley Road.

After all their narrow escapes, nerve-tingling finishes and spectacular victories, Saints finished that one vital point ahead of their arch rivals Wigan, and gave the St Helens club the honour of being crowned the very first winners of the European Super League.

RESULTS

ROUND 19
2, 3 and 4 August

Castleford	16	20	St Helens
Halifax	56	10	Paris S.G.
Leeds	18	56	Bradford
London	20	13	Warrington
Sheffield	12	54	Wigan
Workington	24	30	Oldham

ROUND 20
9, 10 and 11 August

Oldham	14	22	London
Paris S.G.	12	32	St Helens
Sheffield	42	28	Halifax
Warrington	38	24	Castleford
Wigan	68	14	Leeds
Workington	14	28	Bradford

ROUND 21
16, 17 and 18 August

Bradford	26	27	Halifax
Castleford	22	18	Paris S.G.
Leeds	68	28	Workington
London	13	34	Wigan
St Helens	68	2	Sheffield
Warrington	42	24	Oldham

ROUND 22
23, 24, 25 and 26 August

Halifax	64	24	Leeds
London	56	0	Castleford
Oldham	34	25	Sheffield
Paris S.G.	14	27	Bradford
St Helens	66	18	Warrington
Wigan	78	4	Workington

SUPER LEAGUE FINAL STANDINGS

	P	W	D	L	F	A	Pts
St Helens	22	20	0	2	950	459	40
Wigan	22	19	1	2	902	326	39
Bradford Bulls	22	17	0	5	767	409	34
London Broncos	22	12	1	9	611	462	25
Warrington	22	12	0	10	573	565	24
Halifax Blue Sox	22	10	1	11	667	576	21
Sheffield Eagles	22	10	0	12	599	730	20
Oldham Bears	22	9	1	12	473	681	19
Castleford Tigers	22	9	0	13	548	599	18
Leeds	22	6	0	16	555	745	12
Paris St Germain	22	3	1	18	398	795	7
Workington	22	2	1	19	325	1021	5

THE PREMIERSHIP SEMI-FINALS
SEMI-FINAL 1

Simply brilliant

WIGAN 42, BRADFORD BULLS 36
Saturday, August 31
at Central Park, Wigan

Wigan Tries: Edwards (4), Ellison (2), Radlinski, Paul
Goals: Farrell (5)

Bradford Bulls Tries: Bradley (3), Paul (2), Calland, Tomlinson
Goals: McNamara (4)

WIGAN: Kris Radlinski; Danny Ellison, Va'aiga Tuigamala, Gary Connolly, Jason Robinson; Henry Paul, Shaun Edwards; Neil Cowie, Martin Hall, Terry O'Connor, Simon Haughton, Mick Cassidy, Andy Farrell. Substitutes: Kelvin Skerrett, Craig Murdock, Steve Barrow, Andy Johnson

BRADFORD BULLS: Paul Cook; Joe Tamani, Matt Calland, Paul Loughlin, Jon Scales; Graeme Bradley, Robbie Paul; Karl Fairbank, James Lowes, Brian McDermott, Sonny Nickle, Bernard Dwyer, Steve McNamara. Substitutes: Glen Tomlinson, Nathan Graham, Jeremy Donougher, Paul Medley

Referee: Mr D. Campbell (Widnes)
Attendance: 9,878

It was awesome – a sporting contest to rival anything anywhere, as Wigan and Bradford produced a Premiership semi-final of epic proportions.

The Bulls were desperate to make the Final to truly announce their emergence as one of the giants of the British game after a season of such progress. And with coach Brian Smith ready to say his farewells, there was a real buzz around Central Park that something very special was going to happen.

The Bulls did not disappoint. They played superbly – it's just that their excellence proceeded to bring the very best out of Wigan who rose to the challenge superbly in their own quest to salvage some silverware from an otherwise barren season.

The result was a game that seesawed from end to end, featuring no less than 15 tries and none of them gained easily. The skills on show were breathtaking.

Despite the high scores, it was very tough and highly competitive, with no shortage of niggle in the early stages. The ultimate match-winner, Shaun Edwards, might well have seen himself sent off during a fired-up first half. Fortunately for Wigan, not only did Edwards get away with ten minutes in the sin-bin, but also he went on to score four touchdowns.

Brilliant attacking play kept the tries flowing, but the video referee was working overtime, so tight were the decisions as both defences fiercely contested everything. With the aristocratic Paul brothers in direct opposition, almost every attacking play produced something new and innovative. But the man who made the difference was Wigan's Gary Connolly, in his best form of the season and making vital contributions in both attack and defence.

Wigan led 20–16 at half-time, then hit the Bulls with a blitz right after the interval, scoring three brilliant tries in nine minutes. Bradford should have been out for the count, but they displayed incredible commitment and attacking creativity to storm back and draw level at 32–all, and seemed to be on top.

Only when Danny Ellison scored in the 80th minute did Wigan seal victory – but had this game lasted another two minutes who knows what would have happened? Wigan were on their way to Old Trafford and the Bulls were wrapping up their season – such a contrast after a knife-edge game with not a whisker between the two teams.

NO BULL ... Bradford's Paul Cook gets a "don't argue" hand-off from Wigan's explosive Jason Robinson in the epic semi-final at Central Park

SEMI-FINAL 2

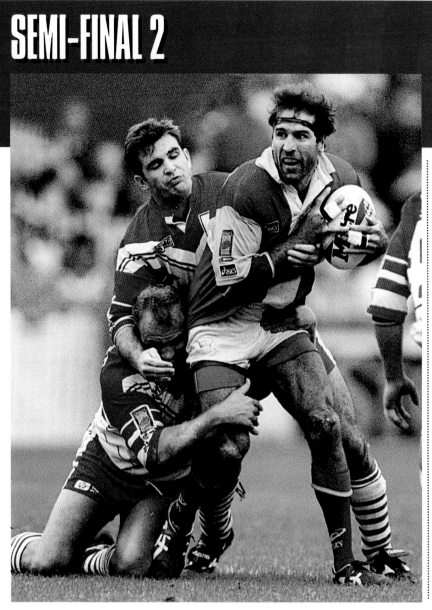

ST HELENS 25, LONDON BRONCOS 14
Sunday, September 1
at Knowsley Road, St Helens

St Helens Tries:	Sullivan (2), Hayes, Goulding
Goals:	Goulding (4)
Drop-Goal:	Goulding

London Broncos Tries:	Strutton (2)
Goals:	Barwick (3)

ST HELENS: Steve Prescott; Joey Hayes, Alan Hunte, Paul Newlove, Anthony Sullivan; Tommy Martyn, Bobbie Goulding; Apollo Perelini, Keiron Cunningham, Adam Fogerty, Chris Joynt, Chris Morley, Karle Hammond. Substitutes: Danny Arnold, Andy Haigh, Derek McVey, Ian Pickavance

LONDON BRONCOS: Tony Martin; Graham Strutton, Greg Barwick, David Krause, Mark Maguire; Tulsen Tollett, Kevin Langer; Gavin Allen, Tony Rea, Tony Mestrov, Peter Gill, Steve Rosolen, Terry Matterson. Substitutes: Russell Bawden, Junior Paul, Darryl Pitt, Leo Dynevor

Referee:	Mr S. Cummings (Widnes)
Attendance:	9,250

TOUGHING IT OUT ... London's Peter Gill tests the St Helens defence as the champions were given a severe work-out

Broncos bruise the Saints

St Helens, having finished top of the Super League, had home field advantage in the Premiership semi-final, but knew they would be in for a very tough game when their opponents emerged as the London Broncos.

The Broncos, having suffered two narrow and controversial defeats at the hands of the Saints in the regular season (and having complained strongly about both), had a real axe to grind. It meant they were really fired up to try to put a damper on the St Helens championship celebrations, and they gave the Saints a real physical mauling.

With big-hitting forwards Tony Mestrov, Steve Rosolen and Russell Bawden

imposing themselves strongly on the game, the Saints found it difficult to get into their customary attacking rhythm. Unable to break that tough defensive line, St Helens had to resort to kicks, and two fumbles by the Broncos produced tries for Joey Hayes and Bobbie Goulding.

London replied with Graham Strutton, who had replaced the injured Martin Offiah, scoring after superb build-up by their centre, Greg Barwick. But, on the stroke of half-time, Anthony Sullivan swooped on another fumble by the Broncos and scored the touchdown that gave his team a 16–8 lead at the break.

London maintained their pressure throughout the second half, and there's little doubt that the intensity of this

game took an awful lot physically out of St Helens – something the Saints paid for a week later in the Final at Old Trafford.

Worst news for St Helens was that Chris Joynt, who was awesome in his battle up front with the Broncos big-hitters, picked up a knee injury. Joynt and Apollo Perelini stood out in a game that saw the St Helens pack tough it out rather than rely on their swashbuckling back-line.

Coach Shaun McRae emphasized the positives, pointing out that 3–0 to his team in games against London was comprehensive enough, but all at Knowsley Road were relieved to see the back of the Broncos for 1996 as they looked ahead to Old Trafford.

THE PREMIERSHIP FINAL

Showdown at Old Trafford

Manchester's Old Trafford stadium bills itself rather grandly as the "Theatre of Dreams", and it provided the perfect backdrop for the final showdown of the 1996 Super League season.

Unfortunately for St Helens, the Stones Premiership Final did not see their dreams come true – their hopes of a hat-trick of major trophies in direct competition with their fiercest local rivals were shattered by a Wigan side absolutely desperate not to lose.

Wigan admitted to being more nervous than normal in the dressing-rooms before this Final. Shaun Edwards, their man who had been there and seen it all before in over a decade of winning big games, knew it was a good sign. Shaun knew his team were going to run hot.

For Wigan, having already watched Saints take the Challenge Cup and the Super League Championship, this was one last throw of the dice – not just to ensure their own season would not end trophy-less, but also to put a severe dent in the ego of the team their fans least wanted to play second-fiddle to.

Saints went into the Premiership Final still licking their wounds from a gruelling physical encounter with the London Broncos seven days before, and with injuries depriving them of powerhouse forwards Chris Joynt and Vila Matautia. Wigan, on the other hand, were bouncing, their confidence boosted by several weeks of top form and after coming out on top in their thrill-a-minute semi-final against the Bradford Bulls.

In front of over 35,000 people at such an impressive stadium, Wigan and St Helens produced yet another game of incredible pace and supreme skills. And it was a game which gave the clearest of examples of how the rules recently introduced to the game have significantly changed the structure of much of the offensive mode of play in Rugby League.

With referees taking the defence back such a big ten yards, and tacklers living in fear of being penalized if they hold on to the man in possession for even a split-second longer than the referee deems acceptable, running from dummy-half has become a key channel of attack at the top level of the game.

WIGAN 44, ST HELENS 14
Sunday, September 9
at Old Trafford, Manchester

Wigan Tries: Ellison (3), Connolly, Edwards, Haughton, Paul, Robinson, Murdock
Goals: Farrell (4)

St Helens Tries: Newlove, Martyn
Goals: Goulding (3)

WIGAN: Kris Radlinski; Danny Ellison, Gary Connolly, Va'aiga Tuigamala, Jason Robinson; Henry Paul, Shaun Edwards; Kelvin Skerrett, Martin Hall, Terry O'Connor, Simon Haughton, Mick Cassidy, Andy Farrell. Substitutes: Neil Cowie, Steve Barrow, Craig Murdock, Andy Johnson

ST HELENS: Steve Prescott; Joey Hayes, Alan Hunte, Paul Newlove, Anthony Sullivan; Tommy Martyn, Bobbie Goulding; Apollo Perelini, Keiron Cunningham, Adam Fogerty, Derek McVey, Chris Morley, Karle Hammond. Substitutes: Danny Arnold, Simon Booth, Andy Haigh, Ian Pickavance

Referee: Mr D. Campbell (Widnes)
Attendance: 35,013

TOUCHDOWN ... Gary Connolly opens the scoring for Wigan in the Premiership Final at Old Trafford after an explosive burst from dummy-half

VICTORY SHOWER ... *Andy Farrell is drenched by his team-mates as Wigan deny Saints a clean-sweep of all the major trophies*

Nobody exploited that better throughout the Super League season than Saints' hooker Keiron Cunningham, who frequently made huge yardage and put his team into good attacking positions.

But Wigan had done their homework and kept Keiron well shackled at Old Trafford. Instead, it was they who cut loose, taking dummy-half running to explosive new heights with, not surprisingly, the master of the art, Jason Robinson, leading the charge.

Perhaps not quite so predictably, bearing in mind his more silky laid-back running style, Gary Connolly was right up there alongside Robinson in the explosive stakes. Playing against his former club, Connolly looked extra determined to put his stamp on this game and it was he who set the wheels rolling for Wigan as early as the ninth minute when he shot out of the blocks at dummy-half and produced an extraordinary burst of pace to go round

Saints' full-back Steve Prescott and score the opening try.

There were no signs of the blitz that was to follow when outstanding second-rower Derek McVey, also attacking from dummy-half, set up Paul Newlove for St Helens' opening try which, with Goulding's conversion, put them in the lead after a quarter of an hour's play.

It was short-lived. That's when Wigan's electric running – so much of it direct from dummy-half initially – took control, as Farrell, Robinson and Edwards injected their skills into the game in huge doses. At half-time Wigan led 18–8, and by the end of 80 exhilarating minutes they had stormed in for 44 points with just 14 in reply from Saints.

Young winger Danny Ellison had a try hat-trick and described his achievement as a dream come true, while captain Andy Farrell later admitted his team had been so determined to win because "there's no way we wanted Saints to win

all three trophies."

Farrell was awarded the Harry Sunderland Memorial Trophy as the game's most valuable player, but several of his team-mates would have been equally worthy recipients – most notably Jason Robinson and Gary Connolly. Shaun Edwards, the experienced warhorse of Wigan's decade of success, recognized just how important his side's smart tactics had been. "Our running from dummy-half was exceptional," said Shaun, "and under the modern rules that's a really big asset." How true were his words.

St Helens coach Shaun McRae recognized the extra hunger in the Wigan team, admitting that they probably wanted victory more than his own team who had already celebrated a championship win. It had been a great season for McRae and the Saints, but it was Wigan who brought the curtain down in such style at the "Theatre of Dreams".

THE TEAMS

Twelve clubs will contest Super League in 1997 – all with their eyes on the ultimate prize ... the Championship.

As St Helens begin the defence of their crown they know the challenges will come thick and fast. Stones Super League Year Two is made up of ten teams from the game's northern heartlands, five from each side of the Pennines, plus the capital city teams of London and Paris.

This chapter presents fans with an insight into those 12 teams – what makes them tick as they approach the 1997 season, who are their "ones to watch", plus a glance at their past achievements and a nostalgic look at their "men of steel".

Super League Route Master

Whether you'll be travelling with your mates in the back of a Ford Transit van or in a chauffeur-driven stretch limo, if you are intent on following your team around the country (not to mention Paris), urging the lads on to greater things, you'll need a full tank of petrol, a decent road map and this handy guide to the Super League grounds.

Bradford Bulls

Odsal Stadium, Bradford, West Yorkshire
BD6 1BS (Tel. 01274 724573)
Tel. 01274 733899 Fax 01274 724730
Internet: http:\\www.bradfordbulls.co.uk

From M62
- Junction 26 (A58/A638/M606). Follow signs Bradford M606.
- Junction with unclassified road.

- Motorway Terminal Roundabout. Take 2nd exit A6036 (signposted Halifax) into Rooley Avenue for Bradford Bulls ground (on the left)

The massive Odsal Stadium bowl once housed the world record Rugby League crowd. The cinder banks and sleepers are long gone and it's a concrete bowl now. Great venue for summer rugby, as long as it doesn't rain. Easy to get to for travelling fans, just a couple of minutes off the Motorway at Odsal Top. The Bulls have significantly increased catering and merchandising vending sites, and the pre-match entertainment is the best in Super League.

Castleford Tigers

Wheldon Road, Castleford,
West Yorkshire WF10 2SD
Tel. 01977 552674
Fax 01977 518007

From East
- M62 Junction 32 (A639). Follow signs Castleford A639. In 0.8 mile at roundabout take 2nd exit A656. In 0.7 mile at roundabout forward 0.2 mile farther at roundabout, take 3rd exit into Wheldon Road (unclassified) for Castleford Tigers ground (on right).

From West
- M62 Junction 31 (A655). Follow signs for Castleford A655.
- Edge of Castleford at roundabout take 2nd exit. In 1.2 miles at roundabout take 2nd exit. In 0.2 mile at roundabout take 2nd exit into Wheldon Road unclassified for Castleford Tigers ground (on right).

Wheldon Road with a packed crowd is as atmospheric as can be – a quaint little ground, with its amber and black painted wooden grandstand, tight terraces and a railway end – a reminder of how Rugby League grounds always used to be. The Tigers' home is just a stone's throw from the town centre, and for those who like a full day of local culture, a visit to the nearby "Early Bath" pub is recommended.

TONY SMITH ... Castleford's international half-back on the attack

Halifax Blue Sox

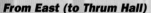

Thrum Hall, Thrum Hall Lane, Halifax,
West Yorkshire HX1 4TL
Tel. 01422 250600
Fax 01422 251666
(Note: Halifax will play some games at
Calderdale Sports Stadium, The Shay, Hunger
Hill, Halifax, HX4 1QT. Tel. as Thrum Hall.)

From East (to Thrum Hall)

- M62 Junction 26 (A58/A638/M606). Follow signs Halifax A58.
- Junction with A641. Forward at crossroads.
- Hipperholme. Forward at traffic lights. By Godley Road enter Halifax.
- At roundabout take 2nd exit then branch left unclassified at T-junction turn right into Pellon Lane. Take 2nd turning left into Bedford Street North. At end turn right into Gibbett Street. In 0.8 mile turn right into Thrum Hall Lane for Halifax Blue Sox ground (on left).

From West (to Thrum Hall)

- Junction A629/M62. Follow signs Halifax, Huddersfield A629.
- Junction with A643. At roundabout take 2nd exit (signposted Halifax) and descend 12%.
- Junction for Elland. In 1.8 miles ascend (1 in 9). In 0.3 mile turn left A646.
- Kings Cross. Turn right A58. In 0.2 mile turn left into Queens Road unclassified. In 0.6 mile at crossroads turn left into Gibbett Street. 0.2 mile farther turn right into Thrum Hall Lane for Halifax Blue Sox ground.

First year at The Shay for Halifax, after over 100 years at Thrum Hall. The Shay, home of Halifax Town Football Club, is much more accessible than Thrum Hall – no steep hills to climb, it's much lower down in the town. An old ground about to be redeveloped into a multi-sport stadium, The Shay has lots of space – perfect for summertime entertainment. Thrum Hall will be the Blue Sox home until June or July.

Leeds Rhinos

Headingley, St Michael's Lane,
Leeds LS6 3BR
Tel. 0113 278 6181
Fax 0113 275 4284

From East

- M62 Junction 29 (M1). Follow signs Leeds M1.
- Junction 43 (A61).
- Junction 47. Leave Motorway and follow signs City Centre.
- LEEDS. Follow signs Otley, Skipton A660 to leave by Woodhouse Lane. In 2.3 miles turn left then left again into St Michael's Lane for Leeds Rhinos ground (on right).

From West

- M62 Junction 27 (A62/A650/M621). Follow signs Leeds M621.

- Junction 1 (A6110).
- Junction 2 (A643). Leave Motorway and at roundabout take 1st exit A643. In 0.8 mile at roundabout take 3rd exit A58. In 0.3 mile branch left and at roundabout take 1st exit into Kirkstall Road A65 (signposted Ilkley). 0.5 mile farther at traffic lights turn right into Willow Road (unclassified). At next crossroads forward into Cardigan Road. In 1 mile turn left into St Michael's Lane for Leeds Rhinos ground.

The Rolls Royce of Rugby League stadiums – not the most modern in the world, but stately and with an air of quality. The main grandstand is double-sided, backing on to the famous Headingley cricket pitch. In the leafy suburbs of Headingley, home to most of the city's student population, this is one ground surrounded by good pubs and food outlets. The stadium itself has superb restaurant facilities on match days.

London Broncos

The Stoop Memorial Ground, Craneford Way,
Twickenham, Middlesex
Tel. 0181 410 5000. Fax 0181 410 5001.
Internet http:\\www.koppanet.com

From outside London

- London Orbital Motorway M25 to junction with M3 (Junction 12/2), go east towards London. M3 becomes A316 but continue towards Twickenham/ London. At roundabout by Twickenham stadium go round until you go back on yourself. London Broncos stadium car parks are on left at 400 yards and 800 yards.

From inside London

- Go west along A4 to Chiswick Roundabout 200 yards beyond Fullers Brewery, Mawson Arms pub. Take exit signposted A316 Richmond, Twickenham, (M3) south west and go approximately 5 miles until Twickenham Stadium looms on your right. London Broncos stadium car parks are on left at 400 yards and 800 yards.

The Stoop Memorial Ground is home of Harlequins Rugby Union club and in the shadow of RFU headquarters at Twickenham. A brand new grandstand has arisen this year, which will dramatically increase restaurant and hospitality facilities. Another stand opposite, seating at one end, provide a neat and compact stadium capable of holding around 10,000 people.

Oldham Bears

Boundary Park, Sheepfoot Lane,
Oldham OL1 2PA (Tel. 0161 624 4972)
Tel. 0161 624 4865 Fax 0161 624 1003
Internet: www.zen.co.uk\oldhambears
E-mail. oldhambears@zen.co.uk

From East/West
• M62 Junction 20. Take A627(M) to junction with A664. Leave Motorway and take 1st exit at roundabout on to Broadway, then 1st right in Hilbre Avenue which leads to car park.

With Watersheddings now just a memory, the Bears have travelled much closer to sea level, to the well-appointed home of the 'Latics. Lots and lots of seats, and covered on all four sides, Oldham will now have one of the best stadiums in Super League.

Paris Saint-Germain

Stade Charlety (Charlety Stadium),
99 Boulevard Kellermann, 75013 Paris
Tel. 00 331 4416 6000 and 00 331 4608 1313
Fax 00 331 4608 3026.

From Britain
• *Eurostar trains:* From Waterloo to Paris Gare du Nord (Tel. 0345 881881).
• *Le Shuttle trains:* From Ashford to Calais.
• *Flights:* Flights from Manchester, Liverpool, Leeds/Bradford and Heathrow, Gatwick, London City, Luton and Stansted to Paris (Charles de Gaulle and Orly airports)
• Coach: National Express. Daily buses from London (Tel. 0990 808080).

In Paris
• *Car parking:* Car parks at Rue Thomire and Avenue Pierre de Coubertin.
• *Trains:* Nearest RER station: Cité Universitaire on line B2 or B4 (Blue line on maps). Runs from Gare du Nord main line station (Tel. (00 331) 45656000). Out of station, turn left and cross road. Stadium is about 500 metres ahead.

• *Buses:* PC 21, 28, 38 and 67 run near the stadium (Tel. (00 331) 43461414).

Road directions
• *From M62:* Take M6, then M1 or A1 to M25 London Orbital Motorway. Head east, go through the Dartford River crossing, and take Junction 2 (signposted A2) for Dover, or take Junction 3 (signposted M20) for Folkestone and Channel Tunnel.
• *From Calais:* Take A16 motorway, follow signs for Paris and turn on to A26 motorway. Pass signs for Arras and turn right on to A1 to Paris. Turn left on to the ring road and take turn off for Porte de Gentilly – Avenue Pierre de Coubertin. Turn right into Boulevard Kellermann, and the PSG ground is on the right.

Undoubtedly the most modern stadium in Super League – it's a state-of-the-art architectural masterpiece for stadium design freaks. Typical of the French. Charlety has 20,000 seats, incredible floodlights and a sensational atmosphere when there's more than 10,000 fans inside. If you're looking for the stadium head for Gentilly – but, don't be too surprised if you get a coolish welcome at the clubhouse bar inside Charlety – it's the home base of P.U.C. (Paris Université Club) Rugby Union!

St Helens

Knowsley Road, St Helens,
Merseyside WA10 4AD
Tel. 01744 23697
Fax 01744 451302

From M62
• Junction 14. Follow signs St Helens (A580). In 1.5 miles join A580.
• Haydock Junction (junction with M6 (Junction 23)). Follow signs Liverpool A580.
• Junction with A58. At traffic lights forward.
• Junction with A571. At traffic lights forward.

• Junction with A570. At traffic lights turn left A570 then turn right B5201. In 1 mile turn left into Mill Brow (unclassified). Shortly forward into Knowsley Road for St Helens ground (on right).

Saints are planning considerable improvements to their ground, but Knowsley Road remains one of the best in the game – a large main grandstand, covered terracing on the opposite side and behind one goal. The club house and restaurant face it. Capacity has been reduced to 17,000 and, as the Super League champions, development of more seats must be a target. Mobile kiosks provide catering, and the Saints club shop can keep you busy for hours.

Salford Reds

The Willows, Willows Road, Weaste,
Salford, Greater Manchester M5 2FT
Tel. 0161 737 6363
Fax 0161 745 8072 Internet:
http:\\www.angel.co.uk\salford

From M62
• Junction 12 (M63/M602). Follow signs Manchester M602.

• Junction with A576. Leave Motorway and at roundabout take 1st exit A576. In 1 mile turn right into Weaste Lane B5228 for Salford Reds ground (on right).

Situated among tightly packed terraced streets, Salford still retains a hint of the old image. The Willows used to shine like a beacon among the darkened red brick. The massive entertainment centre has been refurbished, extensions to the main stand have provided more seats, and the huge north stand looks as imposing as ever. The Reds' home is a compact ground – with the best restaurant facilities.

Sheffield Eagles

Don Valley Stadium, Worksop Road,
Sheffield S9 3TL (Tel. 0114 256 0607)
Tel. 0114 261 0326 Fax 0114 261 0303

From North

- M1 Junction 34 (A6109). Follow signs Sheffield A6109. In 1.4 miles at traffic lights turn left A6102 (signposted Worksop) (A57). In 0.5 mile at roundabout take 2nd exit A6178 (signposted City Centre (A6109)). Sheffield Eagles ground on left.

From South

- M1 Junction 34 (A6178). Follow signs Sheffield (Centre) A6178. In 1.2 miles at roundabout forward (signposted City Centre (A6109)). Sheffield Eagles ground on left.

From Hathersage

- Follow signs Sheffield A625.
- Ecclesall (war memorial).
- Hunters Bar. At roundabout take 2nd exit (signposted City Centre). In 1.1 miles at roundabout take 2nd exit.
- Sheffield. Follow signs Rotherham A6109. In 0.5 mile pass beneath railway arch and bear right. 0.4 mile farther turn right then left (one-way) (signposted Bawtry). Sheffield Eagles ground on right.

It's huge, it's clean, it's modern, it's got great catering facilities and, sadly, it's usually 80 per cent empty. The Don Valley Stadium, developed for the World Student Games, gives the Sheffield Eagles a magnificent home. But all those empty seats don't help the atmosphere – yet the Eagles fans, notably their drummers, can whip up a storm. Just dream what it would be like with 20,000 in there! The athletics track distances the fans from the action.

Warrington Wolves

Wilderspool Stadium, Wilderspool Causeway,
Warrington WA4 6PY
Tel. 01925 635338 Fax 01925 571744

From East

- Junction with M62. Follow signs to Warrington A49. In 0.5 mile at roundabout take 2nd exit. 0.4 mile farther at roundabout take 2nd exit. By Winwick Road enter Warrington.
- Follow signs for Whitchurch A49 to leave by Wilderspool Causeway. Shortly turn left into Fletcher Street (unclassified) for Warrington Wolves ground.

From West

- M62 Junction 7 (A57/A569). Follow signs Warrington A57.
- Junction with A568.
- Great Sankey. In 0.7 mile at roundabout take first exit. By Liverpool Road enter Warrington.
- Follow signs Whitchurch A49 to leave by Wilderspool Causeway. Shortly turn left into Fletcher Street (unclassified) for Warrington Wolves ground.

It used to be surrounded by delightful wooden stands in the days when Brian Bevan was hurtling down the touchline – now Wilderspool is dominated by the huge glass-fronted leisure centre down the length of one side of the pitch, opposite the main grandstand. Warrington's would never claim to be the cosiest or homeliest stadium but facilities are much improved. A capacity of just over 11,000 provides some 2,000 seats.

Wigan Warriors

Central Park, Wigan WN1 1XF
Tel. 01942 231321 Fax 01942 820111

From East

- M61 Junction 5 (A58). Follow signs Wigan A58.
- Hindley. Turn right A577 (signposted Wigan). In 1.5 miles forward into Birket Bank (unclassified). Shortly bear right into Schofield Lane. In 0.3 mile turn left then right into Greenough Street. 0.2 mile farther cross river bridge then turn right into Hilton Street for Wigan Warriors ground.

From North

- M6 Junction 27 (A5209). Follow signs Wigan A5209.
- Standish. At traffic lights turn right A49. By Wigan Lane enter Wigan.
- At roundabout take right turn into Greenough Street. Follow signs Preston A49 round one-way system. In 0.3 mile turn left into Hilton Street (unclassified) for Wigan Warriors ground.

From South

- Junction A49/M6. Motorway Terminal roundabout. Follow signs Wigan A49. In 0.7 mile at roundabout take 2nd exit. By Wallgate enter Wigan. Turn left into Market Street and follow one-way system. In 0.2 mile turn left into Hilton Street (unclassified) for Wigan Warriors ground.

One of Rugby League's most famous grounds and now set for a massive redevelopment. With grandstands down both sides and the new grandstand at what was the old pavilion end, Wigan still only has 5,302 seats out of a capacity of 24,000. The huge Spion Kop end provides much atmosphere when full. Catering facilities should be part of the redevelopment – at the moment it's still just mobile food vans. But you can get a drink in either the Douglas or Sullivan bars. As its name suggests, Wigan's home is dead set in the centre of town, despite the new road systems. In fact, take away Central Park and the middle of Wigan would feel very empty. Plenty of traditional League haunts are just minutes' walk from the ground – notably the Royal Oak and the Griffin (whose "mine host" is one W. J. Boston).

HENRY PAUL ... In the thick of the action

BRADFORD BULLS

Running with the Bulls

No club has seen such a complete and dramatic turnaround in its fortunes over the past 12 months as Bradford. Shaking off their old and staid Bradford Northern image to become the rampant new Bradford Bulls, they embraced the concept of Super League with vigour and promotional flair to rapidly emerge as the game's flagship club.

Bradford's Odsal Stadium was the perfect venue for the launch of summer rugby, in that it was such a forbidding place to visit in the depths of winter that things *had* to be better. But the Bulls pulled off master strokes in their recruitment of Brian Smith as Head Coach and, on Smith's recommendation, Peter Deakin as marketing executive.

Smith overhauled virtually the entire playing staff in preparation for Super League, and when the time came they were ready for lift-off. Of course, Bradford had the enormous boost of qualifying for their first Wembley Final in 23 years on the eve of the first summer season. Although they lost in dramatic fashion to St Helens at Wembley, the Bulls played a full part in what was acknowledged as the greatest ever final, and in it their young captain, Robbie Paul, emerged as one of the game's genuine superstars.

In the Super League Bradford rose to challenge the giants of Wigan and St Helens, beating both in one memorable week in July. The Bulls eventually finished in third place behind those two title challengers and with the highest average crowd in the League. It was heady stuff for the diehard fans who had watched the old Northern slugging it out through a succession of Odsal winters.

The Steam Pigs

Two Bradford clubs were founder members of the Northern Union back in 1895, Manningham, which later became Bradford City soccer club, and Bradford, which eventually became the other soccer club, Park Avenue. The Bradford Northern club was formed in 1907 – they played at Birch Lane until their move to the vast Odsal Stadium in 1934.

During this era Bradford's big pack of forwards rejoiced in the nickname of 'The Steam Pigs' – the name hung around, and became the title of a fanzine in the late 1980s.

Odsal etched its place in Rugby League folklore when it housed the world record crowd in 1954 for a Challenge Cup Final replay– an official figure of 102,575, although reports suggest at least another 20,000 were present.

Bradford's golden era came in the years immediately after World War Two. They reached three successive Challenge Cup Finals at Wembley, the first team to do so, winning in 1947 against Leeds and 1949 against Halifax, but losing in '48 to Wigan. Their captain in those Finals was centre Ernest Ward, who went on to lead his country and to be remembered as one of Britain's finest.

Disaster and revival

But, as if to emphasize how widely the fortunes of sport can change, Bradford hit rock bottom in 1963–64. Attendances in the vast Odsal bowl dropped to a few hundred and the club were forced to pull out of the League in December 1963.

Thankfully, owing to the spirit of quality people like former players Joe Phillips and Trevor Foster, the great revival came in 1964.

ONE TO WATCH

STEVE McNAMARA

Steve McNamara only joined the Bradford Bulls halfway through the 1996 season – and although he made an immediate impression, there's no doubt the best is yet to come from McNamara. Odsal fans are in for a treat, with his skilful ball-handling and ability to push passes sure to set up countless chances for his supporting players. Signed from Hull, and already with Test honours, Mac's a winner for sure.

ODSAL STAMPEDE ... Bulls second-rower Sonny Nickle was a powerful force in 1996

THE BULLS RUN ... Bernard Dwyer, supported by Graeme Bradley, on the run to the London Broncos try-line at The Valley

In the early 1980s coach Peter Fox put together back-to-back Championships for Bradford. An emerging young talent called Ellery Hanley was taking his first steps to stardom at Odsal.

The modern era began at Bradford when Chris Caisley took over as chairman. With Super League on the horizon, Brian Smith was appointed coach and the stampede of the Bulls took the game by storm.

Repeating the success of '96 will be a hard act to follow, the more so because Smith is no longer there. His replacement as coach, Matthew Elliott, has the full confidence of the players, and off the field the club continues to grow. Elliott has set some simple goals: win every game, ensure improvement as individuals and as a team, and have fun.

It's a great time to be a Bradford fan!

Name	Bradford Bulls
Entered League	1895 as "Bradford", re-founded as Bradford Northern in 1907
Colours	White with red, amber and black trimmings, black shorts
Stadium	Odsal Stadium (Capacity 24,000)
Head Coach	Matthew Elliott

CLUB RECORDS

Highest score for	76–0 vs. Leigh East, 1991
Highest score against	18–75 at Leeds, 1931
Most tries in a match	7 by Jim Dechan vs. Bramley, 1906
Most goals in a match	14 by Joe Phillips vs. Batley, 1952
Record home attendance	69,429 vs. Huddersfield, March 1953. Odsal held a world record crowd of 102,569 for a Challenge Cup Final replay between Halifax and Warrington in 1954.

CLUB HONOURS

Rugby League Championship	1903–04, 1939–40, 1940–41, 1944–45, 1979–80, 1980–81
Challenge Cup	1906, 1944, 1947, 1949

MEN OF STEEL

ERNEST WARD

Ernest Ward earned the fitting reputation of being a "gentleman" of Rugby League. He captained Bradford in their three consecutive Wembley Finals in 1947, 1948 and 1949, and went on to become one his country's most respected skippers – touring with the Lions in 1946 and 1950, the latter tour as captain. He played in 15 major finals for Bradford and kicked over 500 goals for them – in later years he was a leading figure in the Bradford and British Lions Players' Associations, and in 1987 the Ernest Ward Memorial Trophy was created in association with Open Rugby and presented to Britain's top international.

CASTLEFORD TIGERS

Tigers eye the prize

Castleford are going to be dangerous opponents in 1997 and the rest of the League had better know it. The Tigers may not quite be wounded animals, but they definitely have some points to prove to the League officials who have too often referred to them as "small town" or "unfashionable".

Cas fans, already angry at the earlier suggestions that their team should be swallowed up into a combined "Calder" team, have got fed up with people questioning their right to be in a Super League. Castleford is a town with Rugby League running through its veins, with a proud history and tradition to match anybody's, and a record of success that several so-called "bigger" clubs might envy.

Look for the Tigers to come out snarling this season. Strengthened by a batch of new signings from Australia, with Lee Crooks ready for one last big fling at the top level and Brendon Tuuta inspiring his colleagues to go forward, Castleford are going to be hard to beat.

LEADING THE WAY ... Castleford Tigers' skipper Lee Crooks looks to set up an attack as he is tackled against the Sheffield Eagles in Super League

Increasing profile

But then Cas have never had too many problems in putting good football teams on the field at Wheldon Road. Their major target now is to increase the profile and commercial activity of the club and fully embrace the Super League concept.

Castleford's chief executive, Richard Wright, sees his mission in 1997 to "increase the profile of the club in Castleford's surrounding areas and make each match day a major event. Increased integration with the community will build spirit and attendances."

Coach John Joyner isn't making any predictions. He's seen considerable team-strengthening in the off-season, and is simply looking for more success in both League and Cup.

Joyner has made a successful transition from player to coach, and acknowledges the know-how he gained from Queenslander Darryl Van de Velde, who brought a new aura of professionalism to Castleford when he became their coach in 1988.

It was while Van de Velde was in charge that Cas made the significant change from homespun club, largely dependent on its own local juniors, to big-spenders, paying large transfer fees to attract ready-made stars.

Biggest of these was Graham Steadman, recruited from neighbours Featherstone Rovers for a then record fee

of £170,000, followed by Lee Crooks, signed from Leeds. Both are still at Wheldon Road, with Crooks the club captain as they embark on Super League year two.

The amber and black

Castleford entered the Rugby League in 1926 after many years as an outstanding team in the Yorkshire Senior Competition. Just nine years after joining the League, Cas were Wembley winners, captained by their famous international centre, Arthur Atkinson.

But they had to wait until the "swinging sixties" before sustained glory days came and Castleford established themselves as one of the game's top clubs. Their inspiration was the half-back pairing of Alan Hardisty and Keith Hepworth. When they were joined later by blockbusting young forwards like Brian Lockwood and Malcolm Reilly, alongside the wily skills of Johnny Ward and Dennis Hartley, the amber and black colours were triumphantly waved at a succession of big games.

Cas were back-to-back Wembley winners in 1969 and '70 before Malcolm Reilly blazed his own personal trail to Australia. When Reilly returned as coach five years later, he guided Castleford back to a place among the elite,

culminating with victory in the 1986 Challenge Cup Final over Hull K.R.

The Tigers' record in the game stands proud comparison with any of their Yorkshire rivals – and they'll be big game hunting again in 1997.

Name	Castleford Tigers
Entered League	1926
Colours	Amber and black
Stadium	Wheldon Road (Capacity 11,750)
Head Coach	John Joyner

CLUB RECORDS

Highest score for	94–12 vs. Huddersfield, 1988
Highest score against	12–62 at St Helens, 1986
Most tries in a match	5 by Derek Foster vs. Hunslet, 1972; John Joyner vs. Millom, 1973; Steve Fenton vs. Dewsbury, 1978; Ian French vs. Hunslet, 1986; and St John Ellis vs. Whitehaven, 1989
Most goals in a match	17 by Sammy Lloyd vs. Millom, 1973
Record home attendance	25,449 vs. Hunslet, March 1935

CLUB HONOURS

Challenge Cup	1935, 1969, 1970, 1986

HALIFAX BLUE SOX

Plenty of Sox Appeal

Halifax have rarely felt as optimistic about a new season as they do about 1997. The Blue Sox are widening their appeal throughout the Calderdale community, and with new signings on the pitch and just as much team strengthening among the back-room staff, Halifax are very serious about their title challenge.

Naturally, their Australian head coach Steve Simms sees the World Club Championship section of Super League as a great opportunity to test his team's standards against Aussie opposition. Simms has become one of the most respected coaches in the British game, one always able and willing to help promote the game in general via his media work.

Last season, after a shaky start, the Blue Sox emerged as one of the best teams in the competition. They aim to be even better in 1997 thanks to some

Name	Halifax Blue Sox
Entered League	1895
Colours	Blue and white
Stadium	Thrum Hall/The Shay (Capacity 12,000)
Head Coach	Steve Simms

CLUB RECORDS

Highest score for	82–8 vs. Runcorn, 1920
Highest score against	0–64 at Wigan, 1923
Most tries in a match	8 by Keith Williams vs. Dewsbury, 1957
Most goals in a match	14 by Bruce Burton vs. Hunslet, 1972
Record home attendance	29,153 vs. Wigan, March 1959 (at Thrum Hall)

CLUB HONOURS

Rugby League Championship	1902–03, 1906–07, 1964–65, 1985–86
Challenge Cup	1903, 1904, 1931, 1939, 1987

SAMOAN FLAIR ... Full-back Mike Umaga is one of a whole batch of South Sea Islanders who sets the Halifax Blue Sox fans abuzz

BLUE SOX HALIFAX R.L.F.C.

shrewd recruitment – most notably Martin Pearson from Featherstone and the vastly experienced Kelvin Skerrett from Wigan.

Pearson is seen as a symbolic signing by Halifax, a statement of their intent to be up with the best in Super League. The skilful stand-off, once on the fringe of the Great Britain team, cost £100,000, and Blue Sox Chief Executive Nigel Wood confirmed it was a significant move by the club. "Just a few years ago we had a reputation for making big money signings, but for the last 18 months we haven't been able to compete at the top end of the transfer market. This is the first time the club has felt secure enough and confident enough about the future to speculate in that market."

All change

It will be all change for Halifax in 1997. Two of Rugby League's oldest and greatest traditions won't accompany 'Fax – their famous blue and white hoops have been replaced by a new kit, and Thrum Hall is no longer home. Halifax are moving to play at The Shay, the soccer ground across town. Thrum Hall will still host early-season Super League games and Academy and Alliance matches, but plans to develop The Shay into a top stadium will go hand in glove with Halifax's future in Super League.

The club, founded in 1873, had been playing at Thrum Hall since 1886. Their reputation as one of the traditional giants of Rugby League was established after World War Two, although it is likely that those war years robbed Halifax of some of their greatest triumphs. They had won the Challenge Cup in 1939 and looked set to stay at the top.

Giants they were, but Halifax always seemed to be the bridesmaids, never the bride. In the space of seven years, between 1949 and 1956, they lost no less than three Wembley Finals (plus a replayed final one famous night at Odsal in front of over 102,000 people) and three Championship Finals.

Glory finally came when Halifax won the Championship in 1965.

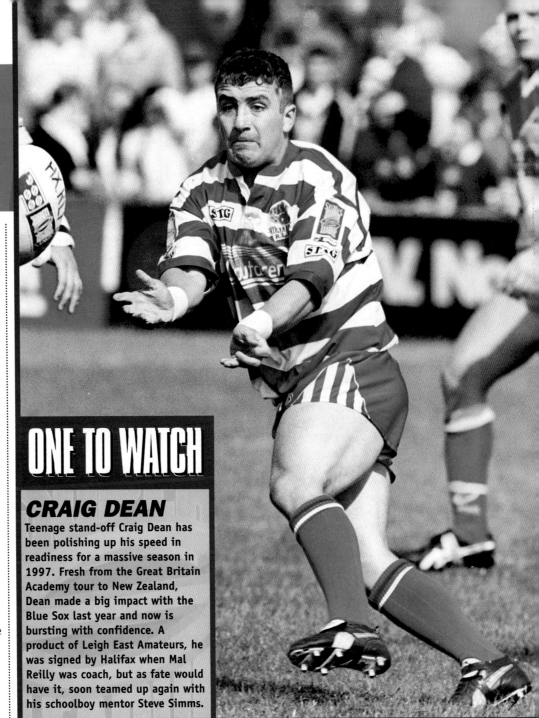

ONE TO WATCH

CRAIG DEAN

Teenage stand-off Craig Dean has been polishing up his speed in readiness for a massive season in 1997. Fresh from the Great Britain Academy tour to New Zealand, Dean made a big impact with the Blue Sox last year and now is bursting with confidence. A product of Leigh East Amateurs, he was signed by Halifax when Mal Reilly was coach, but as fate would have it, soon teamed up again with his schoolboy mentor Steve Simms.

Aussie invasion

The return of Halifax to the elite of the game after long years of struggle came when club president David Brook embarked on a spectacular team-building campaign from Australia.

With former Kangaroo winger Chris Anderson as player-coach, the turnaround in the club's fortunes was quite spectacular. In 1986 Halifax won the Division One Championship, and a year later the Challenge Cup at Wembley.

Now with Steve Simms at the coaching helm and David Hobbs as the new football manager, progress has been more steady, and is being built on firmer foundations. As they embark on a new era at The Shay, Halifax have every reason to be optimistic.

MEN OF STEEL

COLIN DIXON

Colin Dixon joined Halifax as a shy young teenager from South Wales, and ended up becoming one of the town's favourite sons – afforded a hero's farewell when he tragically passed away in 1993. Centre and second-rower Dixon starred for Halifax before joining the Championship-winning Salford side for a then record fee of £12,000. He played in 14 internationals for Great Britain, including victory in the 1972 World Cup, and later returned to coach his beloved Halifax.

LEEDS RHINOS

Name	Leeds Rhinos
Entered League	1895
Colours	Blue and amber
Stadium	Headingley (Capacity 27,500)
Head Coach	Dean Bell

CLUB RECORDS

Highest score for	102–0 vs. Coventry, 1913
Highest score against	6–74 at Wigan, 1992
Most tries in a match	8 by Fred Webster vs. Coventry, 1913; Eric Harris vs. Bradford, 1931
Most goals in a match	13 by Lewis Jones vs. Blackpool, 1957
Record home attendance	40,175 vs. Bradford, May 1947

CLUB HONOURS

Rugby League Championship	1960–61, 1968–69, 1971–72
Challenge Cup	1910, 1923, 1932, 1936, 1941, 1957, 1968, 1977, 1978

Rhinos on the rampage

The first season of summer rugby at Leeds was a major disappointment, both for coach Dean Bell and thousands of Headingley fans. But they could hardly have envisaged the massive changes that were to take place at the Leeds club in time for them to approach 1997 as a whole new ball game.

One of Rugby League's most famous clubs, at certainly its most famous venue, has undergone major surgery in search of that Holy Grail – success!

Leeds have new owners and a new nickname. Wealthy Yorkshire property developer Paul Caddick and Sheffield Eagles founder Gary Hetherington are the new owners. And Leeds are now the Rhinos. Despite a poll among supporters revealing that the majority of them wanted to stick with the Loiners nickname, Rhinos was adopted for marketing reasons.

But can the Rhinos rampage in 1997? Certainly there's new talent in the blue and amber – among a posse of recruits from Australia is the very experienced former St George hooker Wayne Collins, and Hetherington has persuaded talented young Eagles Ryan Sheridan and Dean Lawford to accompany him up the M1 from Sheffield.

Sleeping giants

Leeds haven't won a Championship since 1972 or the Challenge Cup since 1978, and in the ensuing years of frustration endured by their most loyal fans the catch-cry has always been: "If Leeds were really successful they'd get by far the biggest crowds in Rugby League." Not many would disagree – Leeds is a vibrant city, with massive commercial resources. Twenty-thousand crowds at Headingley would be the norm.

But achieving that success, awakening the sleeping giants, has proved an elusive goal for a succession of Leeds coaches. Dean Bell pretty much had his hands tied last season. Now with the impetus of new ownership and the availability of money for player recruitment, Dean should have more chance to get on with the job as he would like.

His fellow New Zealander, Hugh McGahan, has left Leeds to take up a position with Super League in his

LEEDS VICTORY ... The Rhinos defence, here holding up PSG's Laurent Lucchese, will be vital to Leeds' ambitions in '97

RHINO POWER ... *The Leeds pack is about to take possession of the ball at the scrum against the Broncos*

homeland, with Hetherington taking the hands-on management role.

Dean Bell sees his objectives as: "To be challenging for honours in all competitions and to have structures in place that will benefit the club for many years to come." And Leeds certainly have a fine crop of talented teenagers emerging at Headingley – many were thrown in at the deep end last year.

Headingley quality

Leeds were founder members of the Northern Union, and Headingley has always been associated with bringing quality to the game. Players recruited from all over the world have mixed with the best Yorkshire locals to produce many fine sides playing in the famous blue and amber colours.

As far back as the 1930s, when Cumbrian full-back Jim Brough linked with Aussies such as Eric Harris ("The Toowoomba Ghost"), Vic Hey and Jeff Moores, Leeds were a cosmopolitan outfit. After the war Arthur Clues from Australia and Bert Cook from New Zealand continued the traditions. Then along came the Welsh golden boy, Lewis Jones.

Despite these qualities Leeds had to wait until 1961 to achieve their major ambition – winning the Rugby League Championship. Joe Warham was the coach

ONE TO WATCH

TERRY NEWTON

Terry Newton is a young player with an old head on his shoulders. An English Schools star, a product of the Eccles Amateur Club in Manchester, he originally joined Warrington before later signing for Leeds. After a prolonged contract dispute was sorted Terry went straight into the Leeds first team and made a big impact, as hooker and second-rower, in 1996. He toured with the G.B. Academy, and is ready now to show Headingley why so many clubs were so desperate to sign him as a kid.

and mentor of the team that did it.

In the late 1960s an outstanding new Leeds team won cups and championships under the guidance of another charismatic coach, Roy Francis. With superstars like John Holmes, John Atkinson, Alan Smith, Syd Hynes and Les Dyl as Headingley favourites, Leeds won back-to-back Challenge Cups in 1977 and '78. And that was the last major trophy-winning success Headingley has known.

MEN OF STEEL

JOHN HOLMES

The Ice-man, John Holmes was a favourite of the Headingley fans in a marvellous 22-year career with Leeds. A schoolboy prodigy, he made his debut aged 16 in 1968, and played his last game in April 1990, aged 32. He was a major figure in Leeds' Wembley victories of 1977 and '78 – but as well as a great talent at stand-off, centre or full-back, he was also a great clubman. His 11-year Test career saw him play 27 times for Great Britain and England, including scoring a record 26 points against New Zealand in a 1972 World Cup match.

Sure, there were Yorkshire Cups and Regal `trophies, but the big ones have eluded Leeds despite a Who's Who of top coaches being employed to satisfy the expectations of the club and their supporters.

Now 1997 and the start of a new era beckon the Leeds Rhinos. Super League was made for super venues like Headingley and big city clubs like Leeds – the world stage awaits them.

LONDON BRONCOS

BRONCOS STAR NAME ... Martin Offiah, on his debut for London against Warrington, is the capital's biggest name

Name	London Broncos
Entered League	1980 as Fulham, became London Crusaders in 1991, London Broncos in 1994
Colours	Red and blue quartered body with white cross and yellow sleeves
Stadium	The Stoop Memorial Ground (Capacity 10,000)
Head Coach	Tony Currie

CLUB RECORDS

Highest score for	82–0 vs. Highfield, 1995
Highest score against	6–72 vs. Whitehaven, 1986
Most tries in a match	4 by Mark Riley vs. Highfield, 1993; Mark Johnson vs. Highfield, 1994; Scott Roskell vs. Bramley, 1995; Evan Cochrane vs. Sheffield, 1995; Paul Hauff vs. Workington, 1995; and Shane Vincent vs. Highfield, 1995
Most goals in a match	11 by Steve Guyett vs. Huddersfield, 1988; Terry Matterson, vs. Workington, 1996
Record home attendance	15,013 (as Fulham) vs. Wakefield, February 1981

Broncos make the Capital

As the sole British team now in Super League situated outside the old boundaries of Lancashire, Yorkshire and Cheshire, the London Broncos exclusively carry the Rugby Football League's hopes of creating a national identity.

For years people in Rugby League have dreamed about establishing a real presence for the game in London. Hopes have flickered occasionally, only for the dreams to falter on the backs of those who pay only lip service to expansion and real development.

But all that has changed. Super League needs London and it needs it big time. After all the wonderful euphoria and enthusiasm of the original Fulham club when they entered Rugby League so memorably back in 1980, it needed a major impetus from Australia to make the game get serious about London again. It was the Brisbane Broncos club who decided to rescue the battling London team, to try to mould them in their own highly successful image and make Rugby League work in Britain's capital city.

Barry Maranta, one of the men who launched the Brisbane Broncos, is now chairman of the London club and has seen his new venture make remarkable progress in the short time he has been at the helm in England.

In the play-offs

The Broncos had to lay their foundations on Australian players, and they have imported almost all their team not just from the ranks of their parent club in Brisbane, but from a variety of other sources down-under. Few were household names, but under the determined guidance of their coach Tony Currie, the Broncos made massive strides in 1996.

At the end of a season in which they ran both Wigan and St Helens very, very close, and achieved many notable victories over clubs in traditional areas with much larger playing resources, the Broncos finished in fourth place and so made the play-offs. To become the fourth best team in England so quickly says a lot, either about English standards or the abilities of Aussie players – many with backgrounds largely in reserve-grade.

Tony Currie, the former Brisbane, Queensland and Australia centre who also enjoyed a brief spell with Leeds, is a hard taskmaster. Coming second doesn't sit easy with Currie and the Broncos knew it.

But for the club which grew out of Fulham and then the London Crusaders, and has endured a nomadic and

ONE TO WATCH

ADY SPENCER

Ady Spencer is a rarity at the Broncos – he's English! And he's a Cambridge Blue who's put a career in the City on hold to try and make it as a full-time pro footballer with the Broncos. Spencer was a BARLA Youth international with Woolston before going to Cambridge and excelling as player-coach of the Light Blues Rugby League team. He first gained experience with the old London Crusaders three years ago, but he was with the Broncos at pre-season camp in Queensland and has the talent to make a serious impact in 1997.

MEN OF STEEL

ROY LESTER

Any man with the initials R.L. could hardly go wrong in this game – and Roy Lester showed he really was one guy with a steely determination when he played a crucial role in keeping the old Fulham club alive in their darkest days of the mid '80s. If Roy hadn't showed such enthusiasm and strength, there might not be a London Broncos today. He was coach Reg Bowden's very first signing for the original Fulham team – a real pioneer of League in London if ever there was one.

BUCKING BRONCOS ... London's Scott Roskell bursts clear to score against St Helens

traumatic existence for many years, maintained only by the incredible loyalty and determination of the most dedicated band of supporters in any sport anywhere, the current position represents a heady mixture of delight and dreamland.

Building the future

With Barry Maranta so ambitious for League in London, the Broncos are building a big future. Signing Martin Offiah last year was a significant move – not only did they get the game's highest media-profile player, they also got a born and bred Londoner. The Broncos have youth development programmes now in place, overseen by the vastly experienced former Great Britain captain Bev Risman, which they know will, in time, produce London boys with the skills and athletic qualities to shine in Rugby League.

In the short term, of course, Martin Offiah will continue to find that most of his team-mates have Australian accents. But the qualities shown in 1996 by such as Greg Barwick, Peter Gill and Tony Mestrov, alongside captain Terry Matterson, made London a top-four side.

Their first Super League season was spent at Charlton Athletic's The Valley ground, and the massive upturn in attendances was more than encouraging. However, the high cost of renting The Valley, alongside continuing doubts among Broncos officials about the accessibility and geographical location of the south London stadium, have prompted another move for the 1997 season.

This year the London Broncos will be in action at Harlequins' The Stoop ground, in the shadow of Rugby Union headquarters at Twickenham. Although its capacity isn't big enough to house the mega crowds the Broncos hope to attract, especially when their "big brothers" from Brisbane come to play in the World Club Championship, The Stoop has a brand-new grandstand and the west London venue Mr Maranta thinks best.

Rarely since the balmy days of 1980 has Rugby League's future in London been more exciting and more positive.

OLDHAM BEARS

Bears on the prowl

There's something very different about Oldham in the 1997 season. No Watersheddings! After 107 years at the ground that came to symbolize Oldham Rugby League Club, it is no more. The Bears have moved out and will play at Oldham Athletic's Boundary Park this season as they await the development of a new stadium.

It marks the end of links with their past, as the Bears look only to the future. And they know it's going to be no picnic as they battle to establish their Super League credentials.

Last season Oldham's attendances showed just how much work has to be done to fulfil the Super League vision. Having fought strongly against all suggestions of combining with other teams to form a Manchester "super club" and preferring to go it alone, Oldham now have to stand or fall by their own performances on and off the field.

They've certainly got a lot going for them because Oldham is a town full of Rugby League tradition and vibrant amateur clubs, all producing talented young players year after year. The key, of course, would be getting all those youthful stars to play for their hometown club rather than seeking more lucrative pastures elsewhere – for example, two of the game's precocious superstars, Iestyn Harris and Paul Sculthorpe, both chose to join Warrington rather than their local pro club.

Goodway's hopes

In the two-division era Oldham were no strangers to the yo-yo syndrome, and they know even now that many people see them as strugglers compared to the top clubs. But a closer inspection of the facts and crowd figures will reveal that, apart from the big three of St Helens, Wigan and Bradford – and, if they can start winning, Leeds – Oldham lose nothing in comparison with any other team in Super League. Coach Andy Goodway knows that and is confident the Bears can rattle a few cages this year.

Goodway, a Castleford boy who made his name at Oldham as a player, is an ambitious young coach – widely tipped as one of the best of British. Making Oldham succeed, without a team full of star names, will be a real testament to his qualities as a coach.

It remains a source of regret, and wonderment to old-timers, that Oldham are one of the clubs who have never been to Wembley, despite being, in various eras, recognized as the top club in Rugby League. Oldham have actually won the Challenge Cup three times in their history, but the last time came in 1927, just two years before the Final was moved to Wembley. In more recent times a succession of semi-final defeats added to the folklore of Oldham and their vain search for a trip down Wembley way.

Simply the best

In the mid 1950s there's no doubt that Oldham were seen as one of the best. They won the Championship in 1957, the

Name	Oldham Bears
Entered League	1895
Colours	Red and white jerseys, navy blue shorts
Stadium	Boundary Park (Capacity 13,500)
Head Coach	Andy Goodway

CLUB RECORDS

Highest score for	70–10 vs. Bramley, 1995
Highest score against	11–67 at Hull K.R., 1978
Most tries in a match	7 by James Miller vs. Barry, 1908
Most goals in a match	14 by Bernard Ganley vs. Liverpool City, 1959
Record home attendance	28,000 (at Watersheddings) vs. Huddersfield, 1912

CLUB HONOURS

Rugby League Championship	1909–10, 1910–11, 1956–57
Challenge Cup	1899, 1925, 1927

LOOKING FOR ACTION ... Bears stand-off Francis Maloney has the talent to set Oldham's attack moving and to score some sparkling solo tries himself

ONE TO WATCH

DAVID BRADBURY

This young player really came of age in the first Super League season – being Oldham's most incisive forward and winning selection for the Great Britain touring team. A product of amateur League in Leigh, Bradbury has gained so much experience over the past 12 months he's going to be one of the top loose-forwards in Super League in 1997.

crowning glory for a team inspired by a pack including "Rocky" Turner, Charlie Winslade and Syd Little, scrum-half Frank Pitchford, Test centre Alan Davies, and record goal-kicking full-back Bernard Ganley. Those names are remembered as Oldham legends.

In the 1980s, with Great Britain coach Frank Myler at the helm and a fine crop of local juniors being developed, hopes were high again at Watersheddings. And when Myler took the 1984 British Lions touring team to Australia no less than five Oldham players went with him – Terry Flanagan, Andy Goodway, Des Foy, Ray Ashton and Mick Worrall.

Now the Bears are set to begin their new life away from the Watersheddings. They have a proud history to live up to, and they carry the hopes of a whole town.

MEN OF STEEL

ALAN DAVIES

The most brilliant centre of his generation, Alan Davies made his debut for Oldham in 1950 and went on to play 11 seasons at the Watersheddings before transferring to Wigan. He scored a record 174 tries for Oldham, and became their most capped international with 20 Tests or World Cup games for Great Britain. He played in both the 1957 and 1960 World Cups, and toured with the legendary 1958 Lions, as well as starring for Oldham in their 1957 Championship win.

PARIS ST GERMAIN PSG
RUGBY LEAGUE

Crossing the Channel

Much of the national media focus of the inaugural Super League season surrounded Paris Saint Germain. Rugby League was leading the way, ahead of the other football codes, by including a team based in continental Europe in a previously British competition. This team, bearing the name PSG – one of the world's most famous soccer clubs – attracted immediate attention.

The inclusion of the Paris Saint Germain team in the Super League gave the game in France a much-needed publicity boost. Rugby League has struggled across the Channel for several years, starved of the television and media coverage that are the lifeblood of all sports in this modern age.

Initially put together by Jacques Fouroux and Tas Baitieri, Paris launched Super League with an amazing and emotional first night against the Sheffield Eagles at Charlety Stadium. In the southern suburbs of the city, Charlety is a magnificent modern arena, albeit the most expensive to hire anywhere in Super League. Packed with over 17,000 people, as it was against Sheffield, it was a formidable experience.

Initially the PSG team was made up of players from the French League – a mixture of the best native Frenchmen and overseas imports. The fact that most of them were simultaneously still playing for their local clubs in the domestic competition created a fatigue factor that put Paris at a major disadvantage and brought the team to its knees after much optimism in their earlier performances.

Changing horses

Mid-season changes helped turn things around for Paris. Most significantly, the French competition ended and players were free to concentrate on Super League. Alongside that, Britain's Director of Coaching, John Kear, was drafted in to advise and the playing ranks were boosted by a collection of new imports from Australia – among them the outstanding Dion Bird.

PSG will start their second season in very different shape. Both Jacques Fouroux and Tas Baitieri have gone – Fouroux, frustrated by many aspects, returning to Rugby Union, and Baitieri to Australia.

A new coach from Australia, Peter Mulholland, is at the helm. Formerly at the Western Reds in Perth, Mulholland will have a host of new players coming from Australia with him. In fact, only three Frenchmen will be on PSG's initial roster for 1997 – Pierre Chamorin, Pascal

HANGING IN ... Two of the stalwarts of the PSG pack in year one, Didier Cabestany and Jason Sands, tackle a Workington opponent, with Patrick Entat ready to help

MEN OF STEEL

PATRICK ENTAT

Patrick Entat played in every single game of Paris Saint Germain's tough opening season – and at the same time played for Avignon his home-town club and the French national team. Entat may be small, but he's got plenty of steel in his body. No individual could have put more heart-and-soul effort into trying to lift his team in Super League than Patrick did in 1996. Hopefully, he'll get a little more help in '97, but already, in the one year history of the club, his name has been written into the annals as a rock of Rugby League in Paris.

TAKING THE HIT ... Didier Cabestany absorbed plenty for Paris, this one on opening night against Sheffield Eagles at Charlety

Bomati and Fabien Devecchi. They will be joined by Patrick Entat, Vea Bloomfield and Vincent Wulf – all PSG stalwarts from last season – from French champions Villeneuve, and the rest of the squad is likely to be Australian.

ONE TO WATCH

PASCAL BOMATI

By the end of the first Super League campaign Pascal Bomati was playing with as much confidence as any winger in the game. Playing in a pro competition brought the best out of Pascal's abilities and he finished as PSG's top try-scorer. From the XIII Catalan club in Perpignan, Bomati was only 18 when he played his first Test for France. Slightly built, he was originally a stand-off who progressed to the wing, *à la* Jason Robinson. He's a genuine star who can shine in Paris in '97.

Entat's determination

The Paris squad were spending January in training together in Australia in preparation for Super League Year Two. For Patrick Entat, for so long the courageous heartbeat of French national teams, this promises to be one last throw of the dice. He thrives on the challenge of professional Rugby League and the week-by-week pressure demanded by Super League.

The Paris club in 1997 will be heavily administered by staff appointed by the British League. This year the public will be asked to pay for admission – last year it was free to home fans– and, hopefully, a merchandising programme for the highly successful PSG brand will be adopted by the Rugby League club.

There are also plans for at least two '"home" games during the holiday month of August to be staged at venues in the south of France. This would be a major boost for French Rugby League, taking the game to the people, and boosting the state of the game across the Channel is the greatest service PSG can do.

With only one year behind them,

history and tradition don't figure in the Paris vocabulary – but as representatives of the game in France as a whole they have a marvellous heritage to preserve. They also have the small matter of being entirely responsible for putting the "Euro" into Euro Super League.

Name	Paris Saint Germain
Entered League	1996
Colours	Blue with red and white stripe
Stadium	Charlety Stadium (Capacity 25,000)
Head Coach	Peter Mulholland

CLUB RECORDS

Highest score for	34–12 vs. Workington, 1996
Highest score against	8–76 at Wigan, 1996
Most tries in a match	3 by Pierre Chamorin vs. Workington, 1996; and Régis Pastre-Courtine vs. Warrington, 1996
Most goals in a match	5 by Patrick Torreilles vs. Workington
Record home attendance	17,873 vs. Sheffield, 1996

ST HELENS

Name	St Helens
Entered League	1895
Colours	Red and white
Stadium	Knowsley Road (Capacity 19,000)
Head Coach	Shaun McRae

CLUB RECORDS

Highest score for	112–0 vs. Carlisle, 1986
Highest score against	6–78 at Warrington, 1909
Most tries in a match	6 by Alf Ellaby vs. Barrow, 1932; Steve Llewellyn vs. Castleford, 1956; Steve Llewellyn vs. Liverpool, 1956; Tom Van Vollenhoven vs. Wakefield, 1957; Tom Van Vollenhoven vs. Blackpool, 1962; Frank Myler vs. Maryport, 1969; and Shane Cooper vs. Hull, 1988
Most goals in a match	16 by Paul Loughlin vs. Carlisle, 1986
Record home attendance	35,695 vs. Wigan, 1949

CLUB HONOURS

Super League Championship	1996
Rugby League Championship	1931–32, 1952–53, 1958–59, 1965–66, 1969–70, 1970–71, 1974–75
Challenge Cup	1956, 1961, 1966, 1972, 1976, 1996

Saints and the attacking style

St Helens have a proud achievement written in the record books, and it's something that can never be taken away from them. Saints were the very first champions of the European Super League.

Their achievement in 1996 came after a thrilling season in which the Saints' attacking style, their trademark for so many years, thrived on the firm, dry pitches of summer. St Helens would be the first to admit they had quite a few narrow squeaks along the way, but that only added to the excitement of the chase, and nobody could disagree they were very worthy champions.

It was a year in which St Helens showed that they, as much as any club, were prepared to accept the new challenges of Super League. With former R.F.L. official David Howes as their chief executive, they brought a new professionalism to the organization at Knowsley Road and a new enthusiasm to promoting their club and the game.

Meanwhile, on the field, the recruitment of coach Shaun McRae from Canberra galvanized the Saints and did much to create the backbone of discipline that led to the championship.

McRae was voted Coach of the Year, but wasted little time before looking ahead to the new challenges of 1997. "Our mission is to emulate last season's results, and to continue moving forward with an international Super League flavour for the expansion of our great game," stated the coach.

David Howes, meanwhile, has recognized the opportunities to promote the club to a wider audience: "The promotion of international Super League will help increase the commercial activity of the club, plus we plan to continue improving stadium facilities for the benefit of the game," he said.

Off to Liverpool

Saints already have plans to play their home game against Castleford Tigers in 1997 at Liverpool's Anfield Stadium – a huge opportunity to attract new fans and put the game on a higher level of presentation. But St Helens have always been in the forefront of pushing back the frontiers for the game, ever since they became a founder member of the Northern Union in 1895.

They played in the very first Challenge Cup Final, losing to Batley in

CHALKING IT UP ... Another try for St Helens on their way to the 1996 European Super League championship

MEN OF STEEL

ALAN PRESCOTT

Alan Prescott became a legend in the history of Rugby League when he broke his arm in the opening minutes of the second Test in 1958, but played on to help win the Ashes. As Great Britain's captain he was a hero, as he was back home in St Helens where he skippered Saints to their first Wembley victory in 1956 and won the Lance Todd Trophy. A mighty prop-forward, Prescott played 28 times for Great Britain and 11 times for England, and appeared in nine major finals for Saints.

ONE TO WATCH

JOEY HAYES

The explosive pace and elusive running of Joey Hayes put him on the threshold of becoming a mega-star of Super League in 1997. Sadly, a leg injury might just hold him back for a while, but Joey will bounce back. Recruited from Warrington amateur League, Hayes starred for Saints and Great Britain Academy before being called up by Phil Larder for the 1996 Lions tour. Like the Saints backline as a whole, Joey Hayes spells entertainment!

1897. A century later it was Saints who wrote their name on that most famous old trophy, after Bobbie Goulding had led them to victory at Wembley against the Bradford Bulls.

St Helens really established themselves as a major force in the game in the 1950s. In 1953 they won the Championship, but lost in the Challenge Cup Final at Wembley 15–10 to Huddersfield. The Saints finally got their hands on the Challenge Cup in 1956 when, captained by Alan Prescott, they beat Halifax.

At this time St Helens were building an era that would centre around players who went on to become household names in the folklore of Rugby League – names like Alex Murphy, Vince Karalius, Austin Rhodes, Dick Huddart and Tom Van Vollenhoven, as well as Prescott. In the 1960s the success continued, with players like Cockney Cliff Watson, Tommy Bishop and Len Killeen added to the list of legends at Knowsley Road.

In more recent times St Helens have suffered most from Wigan's domination of British Rugby League. One, because they are fierce local rivals who, even if they were both joint bottom of the second division, would regard winning their derby matches as the most vital event of any season. Two, because throughout the decade, Saints were consistently the team which ran Wigan closest – losing championships on points difference or key games by the odd point.

All that changed in 1996. Bobbie Goulding, Shaun McRae and St Helens were winners. And the Saints don't plan to rest on their laurels. They're using that success as a launching pad to bigger and better things in 1997.

NO HOLDING BACK ... Derek McVey proved a handful for all Saints' opponents in '96

SALFORD REDS

Planning a Red alert

Salford are the team who approach the 1997 season with the most anticipation and probably a little trepidation. This is because, as the promoted side from last year's Division One, they are the only newcomers to the Super League. Has the onset of full-time professionalism caused a massive gap to evolve between the divisions? If so, how will the Reds bridge it in the short term?

These are questions that will only add to the excitement at The Willows, and also add to coach Andy Gregory's thoroughness in preparing his team.

Salford are confident they can handle it – after

all they were the team which ended Wigan's stranglehold on the Challenge Cup in 1996. As Gregory has matured as a coach, so the Reds have progressed as a team, and their pack has been considerably strengthened for '97 by the signings of former internationals Andy Platt and John Cartwright.

Coach Gregory, the former Wigan and Great Britain scrum-half star, is straightforward about his ambitions for 1997. "To continue team-building to ensure that we can compete at both Super League and World Club Championship levels."

REDS DEFENCE ... Salford's power was shown in last season's Division One Premiership Final, with Keighley's Daryl Powell on the receiving end of this mega hit

A major force

Reds' chief executive David Tarry says the aim is: "To re-establish Salford as a major force in Rugby League at both playing and commercial levels."

Note David's emphasis on re-establish, because not so many years ago Salford were the number one club in the game. The very first winners of the Championship after the League split into two divisions in 1973–74, the Reds repeated that feat two seasons later. Commercially, they were streets ahead of any rival club. At a time when the game was enduring a rather depressed era, with small crowds and a lack of flair and enthusiasm, Salford shone like a beacon.

The catalyst for that success was their charismatic chairman, Brian Snape, who, by developing the facilities at The Willows and spending big money in the transfer market to secure the best League players available and a host of successful converts from international Rugby Union, made Salford the place to be in Rugby League.

They were called the Red Devils then and their inspiration was the side which originally coined that famous nickname back in the 1930s. That was Salford's previous golden age and holds a very special place in the history of Rugby League. Their mentor was manager Lance Todd, one of the great names in the game's heritage, a name celebrated every year in the Wembley Final when the man-of-the-match wins the Lance Todd Trophy. And their captain was Gus Risman, another immortal.

The actual Red Devils nickname originated when Salford helped to pioneer Rugby League in France. The French fans, so grateful for their assistance in making their tour and so impressed by the quality of their play, described them as "Les Diables Rouges" and the name stuck.

STYLISH STAND-OFF ... Salford's Steve Blakely is looking forward to Super League

ONE TO WATCH

DARREN ROGERS

The Salford Reds bring an exciting three-quarter line to Super League in 1997, and watch out for big winger Darren Rogers. A strong runner and prolific finisher, Darren will relish the challenge of testing himself against the best. He was a Great Britain Academy international with Dewsbury before crossing the Pennines to join the Reds, and he's one of the new names looking to emerge in '97.

Name	Salford Reds
Entered League	1895
Colours	Red with black and white trimmings, white shorts
Stadium	The Willows (Capacity 11,111)
Head Coach	Andy Gregory

CLUB RECORDS

Highest score for	78–0 vs. Liverpool, 1907
Highest score against	6–70 at Wigan, 1993
Most tries in a match	6 by Frank Miles vs. Leeds, 1898; Ernest Bone vs. Goole, 1902; and Jack Hilton vs. Leigh, 1939
Most goals in a match	13 by Gus Risman vs. Bramley, 1933; Gus Risman vs. Broughton Rangers, 1940; David Watkins vs. Keighley, 1972; and Steve Rule vs. Doncaster, 1981
Record home attendance	26,470 vs. Warrington, February 1937

CLUB HONOURS

Rugby League Championship	1913–14, 1932–33, 1936–37, 1938–39, 1973–74, 1975–76
Challenge Cup	1938

Simply red

Now known simply as the Reds, Salford are delighted to be back in the elite of the game. Andy Gregory is rated one of the best emerging British coaches, recognized by his appointment with the Great Britain World Nines team, and he has some fine talent to work with.

Off the field, Salford are spending a considerable amount of money to improve stadium facilities. Work to their main grandstand has provided two new wing sections with a combined total of 1,200 seats, plus extra disabled facilities. Complete refurbishment of the giant North Stand is in hand, too. And, having made great efforts to attract families and youngsters, the Reds are making ladies' facilities a high priority this season.

For the Salford Reds, so ambitious and so determined to succeed, this is an exciting time.

MEN OF STEEL

GUS RISMAN

A founding member of Rugby League's Hall of Fame, Gus Risman had an incredible 25 years in first-class football, stretching from 1929 to 1954. Whilst his later feats in player-coaching Workington Town to such success have become legendary, Salford was the club for which Risman starred in the first major section of his career – captaining them to Wembley victory in 1938 and three Championships in the '30s, under the managership of Lance Todd. Risman scored over 2,000 points in 427 games for the Red Devils, made three Lions tours, the last in 1946 as captain, and played in five winning Ashes Test series.

SHEFFIELD EAGLES

Eagles take new flight path

Please pardon the Sheffield Eagles players and fans if they feel that something is missing when they run out for their opening game of Super League 1997. Not something, but somebody!

After being there throughout the Eagles' history, Gary Hetherington has moved out to become part-owner of Leeds. He was the man who founded the Sheffield club and at some time had been its chairman, manager, coach, spokesman and just about everything else you can think of, so life without Hetherington is bound to be a little strange for a while.

But the Eagles haven't let the grass grow under their feet, and start the rest of their lives with probably the strongest coaching team anywhere in the British game. Phil Larder, the 1996 Great Britain coach, has taken over as head coach of the Eagles, and working alongside him will be John Kear, the man who succeeded Larder as National Director of Coaching.

Both Larder and Kear have hands-on experience at the very top level of international football and were also involved with clubs last season – Larder with the Keighley Cougars and Kear with Paris Saint Germain.

They will find an Eagles set-up with batteries recharged by the influx of new blood and new leadership – and that's no disrespect at all to Gary Hetherington, who worked wonders in keeping the club afloat in its early days and, eventually, making it such a success.

At the Don Valley

Sheffield will, after all, still be playing at the Don Valley Stadium, despite earlier announcements that they were to move to Sheffield United's Bramall Lane. And coach Phil Larder is more than happy with his import recruits from the Australian Super League player-pool.

Having lost Ryan Sheridan to Hetherington's Leeds, the Eagles will be looking to their playmakers, Johnny Lawless and Mark Aston, to give them a lead. And coach Larder is more than happy to have Test prop Paul Broadbent leading their pack.

Sheffield, with their new coaches and new players, show every sign of being one of the biggest improvers of Super League. What they lacked last year was

EAGLES ATTACK ... Hooker Johnny Lawless sets the line moving against Castleford

MEN OF STEEL

DARYL POWELL

In the steel city look no further than Daryl Powell as the original rock of the Eagles. Powell was Sheffield's very first signing back in 1984 and, boy, did they get value for money from this former Redhill amateur. He served the Eagles for 11 years, captaining them to all their major victories, establishing appearance records and becoming the club's very first international. He went on to become one of Great Britain's most capped players, featuring in 33 Tests, the last on the 1996 Lions tour.

SHOELESS IN SHEFFIELD ... Nothing upsets the concentration of Paul Carr, an outstanding servant to the Eagles

consistency.

The Eagles are one of the game's youngest clubs, and have shown that, whilst overnight success can be bought by huge amounts of money, lasting success and strong foundations only come from hard work and steady development.

Sheffield knew there would be no instant success for them when they joined the League in 1984 and promptly found that their major financial backer had gone bust. Instead it meant a hand-to-mouth existence at cold and cavernous Owlerton Stadium, and sensible recruitment from the local Yorkshire amateur clubs to unearth players. It's a tribute to Gary Hetherington's abilities that they hung in and succeeded.

Glory came in 1989 when the Eagles won promotion to Division One, but they could not hang on to their elite status. Instead, after relegation, they went on to win the Second Division Premiership at Old Trafford – Sheffield's first major honour. The Eagles by this time had built a reputation for signing and developing young talent from under the noses of their longer-established Yorkshire rivals – most notably Daryl Powell, their first international player, Mark Aston, David Mycoe and Anthony Farrell.

A great servant

One of their best-ever signings was Mick Cook, a hooker-cum-loose-forward from the Leeds Amateur League. He's been with the Eagles through thick and thin, and was awarded a three-month testimonial at the start of 1997.

The Eagles first moved into the Don Valley Stadium – the venue for the World Student Games – in 1990 and they fulfil all the credentials for Super League's vision – a big city, known throughout the world, and a superb, modern stadium. But, despite excellent media coverage and a very positive high profile in the city, Rugby League in Sheffield has yet to attract the kind of crowds the game would like.

More success in '97 will, hopefully, start to change all that for the better.

ONE TO WATCH

KEITH SENIOR

Keith Senior came from nowhere to emerge as one of Sheffield's stars in Super League 1996, so much so that he won selection for the Great Britain Lions tour. Signed from amateur League in Huddersfield, the tall, rangy Senior proved a handful for opposition defences. With experience of a tour behind him, 1997 will be a very big year for Senior in an Eagles side boosted by new talent and new coaches.

Name	Sheffield Eagles
Entered League	1984
Colours	Red, gold and white jerseys
Stadium	Don Valley Stadium (Capacity 25,000)
Head Coach	Phil Larder

CLUB RECORDS

Highest score for	80–8 vs. Wigan St Patrick's, 1988
Highest score against	2–80 vs. Australians, 1994
Most tries in a match	5 by Daryl Powell vs. Mansfield, 1989
Most goals in a match	12 by Roy Rafferty vs. Fulham, 1986; Mark Aston vs. Keighley, 1992
Record home attendance	8,636 vs. Widnes, October 1989 (at Bramall Lane)

WARRINGTON WOLVES

Dancing with the Wolves

Warrington went within a whisker of attaining a top-four place last season. In a nutshell, they aim to go at least one better in 1997 and make the play-offs.

And the newly named Wolves have impressed many observers with the quality of their off-season recruits, notably the New Zealanders Nigel Vagana, Dallas Meade and Tony Tatupu.

Warrington coach John Dorahy is particularly delighted by the signing of quality young players like Vagana. Dorahy said: "He, in my view, epitomizes what being a player is all about. He's got a relaxed attitude, but he's got great skills and defensive strength. It's a pleasure for a coach to have people of this calibre at the club."

Fulsome praise from coach Dorahy, who, despite his reputation as "Joe Cool", has found it hard to suppress the bubbling enthusiasm that overtook everybody at Wilderspool in the build-up to the 1997 season.

Like all the Australian coaches with British clubs, Dorahy is excited by the challenge of the World Club Championship games and the chance for his team to test themselves against Aussie clubs.

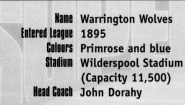

Name	Warrington Wolves
Entered League	1895
Colours	Primrose and blue
Stadium	Wilderspool Stadium (Capacity 11,500)
Head Coach	John Dorahy

CLUB RECORDS

Highest score for	78–6 vs. St Helens, 1909
Highest score against	0–80 at St Helens, 1996
Most tries in a match	7 by Brian Bevan vs. Leigh, 1948; and Brian Bevan vs. Bramley, 1953
Most goals in a match	14 by Harold Palin vs. Liverpool, 1950
Record home attendance	34,304 vs. Wigan, January 1949

CLUB HONOURS

Rugby League Championship	1947–48, 1953–54, 1954–55, 1973–74 (Merit Table)
Challenge Cup	1905, 1907, 1950, 1954, 1974

KIWI POWER ... Richard Henare, on the attack for Warrington against Workington, is just one of a stack of New Zealanders at Wilderspool

ONE TO WATCH

NIGEL VAGANA

Warrington coach John Dorahy is delighted to have Nigel Vagana on his team for 1997. The 21-year-old New Zealander was tipped to be a star this year for the Auckland Warriors, but instead he opted for Wilderspool and the European Super League. He was in Western Samoa's World Cup squad, was a Junior Kiwi and starred for the Warriors' reserve-grade team who reached their Grand Final. Expect him to be one of the major new faces of the 1997 season.

Murphy's charisma

A major factor in the feel-good glow of Warrington is the charisma of football manager Alex Murphy. There's never a dull moment with Alex around. He's still fondly remembered at Wilderspool for his deeds as a player-coach who won the Challenge Cup for Warrington in 1974.

Chief Executive John Smith says the whole mood at the club is positive in 1997: "We are going forward in 1997, and our aim is to build the image of the club [the change of nickname from Wire to Wolves was made during the off-season] and to market that aggressively with a view to significantly increasing attendance levels."

Alex Murphy was in fine verbal form in the build-up to the '97 season, claiming, "I've got a board of directors, for the first time in my life, which wants to go forward on the field." For a man who's been in the pro game for over 40 years that may tell a story, but it's the kind of comment typical of Alex, so adept at firing up the media and the public.

Of all the clubs in Super League, Warrington are looking forward so enthusiastically that they appear to be the club least likely to reflect on past glories. But this is a club with a long and proud history.

Another founder member of the Northern Union, they appeared in three Challenge Cup Finals in the first five years of the century. But their real golden era came in the decade after World War Two – inspired by two Australians, forward Harry Bath and the

IN THE WAR-ZONE ... Front-rower Mark Hilton makes the hard yards for Warrington against Leeds and is always where the going is toughest

legendary wingman, Brian Bevan. Bevan hardly looked like a Rugby League player but his try-scoring feats were incredible.

Double winners

Amongst several Cup and Championship victories in that era, Warrington won the double in 1954, the Challenge Cup being clinched in the famous Odsal replay in front of a world record crowd.

The primrose and blue colours flew high again in the Murphy-coached era of the 1970s. In more recent times Warrington have become well known and respected for their youth development policy which has established a scouting system that attracts top juniors from all over the BARLA network.

John Dorahy and his team aim to make the Wolves feared throughout the Super League – not just in England but down-under, too.

MEN OF STEEL

BRIAN BEVAN

Brian Bevan was just about the most astonishing man ever to play Rugby League. From Sydney, he played trials for Warrington whilst serving with the Australian Navy in 1945. Despite a frail and spindly appearance, which belied his youth and athleticism, Warrington liked what they saw and Bevan returned to a sensational career that saw him become the greatest try-scorer in the history of the game. His mind-blowing tally came to 796 tries in 688 first-class matches. Bevan never got to play a Test for his native Australia, but he starred for the Other Nationalities team and was an original member of the Rugby League Hall of Fame.

WIGAN WARRIORS

Peerless giants of the game

The 1996 season brought a strange feeling to the fans and players at Central Park, Wigan. For the first time in almost a decade Wigan were not picking up the Challenge Cup or the Championship trophy. The giants of the game were having to make do without either of those pieces of silverware in their trophy cabinet after a sensational run of eight consecutive Challenge Cups and six consecutive doubles.

Wigan's dynasty dominated British Rugby League as never before in the decade before the launch of Super League, but the club has rarely been out of the limelight as one of the game's leading forces throughout its 100-year history.

They were one of the founder members of the inaugural Northern Union back in 1895, and have subsequently won more cups and championships and provided more Great Britain internationals than any other club.

ONE TO WATCH

CRAIG MURDOCK

Stepping into shoes as big as those of Shaun Edwards, the man at the hub of Wigan's decade of glory, is the ultimate challenge for any young player. But Craig Murdock, signed in August 1993 from Whitehaven amateur club Hensingham after starring for the BARLA Young Lions, has bided his time and answered the call to first-team duty whenever it has arisen. Twenty-two-years-old Murdock has shown he has the talent and skills to be a star in his own right.

MEN OF STEEL

BILLY BOSTON

Central Park, Wigan, has been a home to the top stars of Rugby League for almost a century, but among the host of heroes none stands out more to the Wigan public than Billy Boston. Billy played for Wigan from 1954 to 1968, scoring a club record of 478 tries in 487 appearances in the cherry and white. He was one of the founder inductees to Rugby League's Hall of Fame, after playing in 31 internationals for Great Britain. Truly a legend among legends at Wigan.

Central Park opened

Their Central Park ground, opened in September 1902, has stood as a focal point for the town of Wigan, and also been the venue of many famous Test matches and cup finals over the years.

The cherry and white colours of Wigan have seen many great sides in the different eras of the game. In the early days of the century the legendary New Zealander, Lance Todd, was recruited and was a major inspiration.

In the 1930s Welshman Jim Sullivan dominated Central Park like a colossus, after he captained Wigan to the very first Challenge Cup Final to be played at Wembley in 1929. And in the years immediately after the Second World War another great Wigan dynasty emerged, with Sullivan as coach and inspirational players like Joe Egan, Ken Gee, Martin Ryan and Tommy Bradshaw at the hub.

By the late 1950s another outstanding Wigan team had been moulded which took them to five Wembley finals in seven years. Captained by Eric Ashton, this Wigan side included the legendary Billy Boston, stand-off

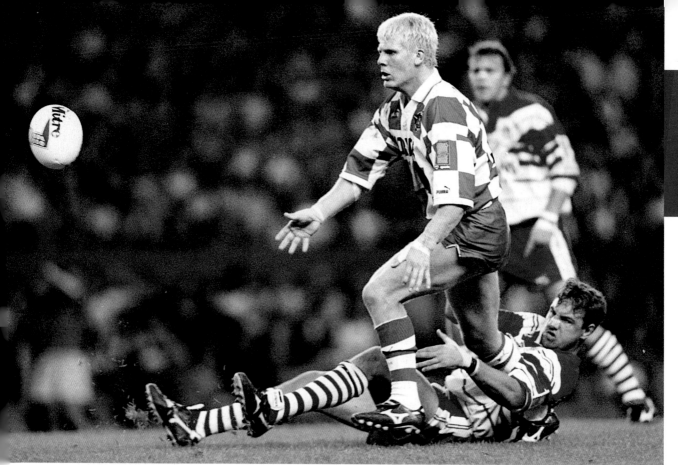

NEVER GIVE UP ... That is the motto of Wigan's Mick Cassidy, pictured in the 1996 Premiership Final victory over St Helens

David Bolton and forwards like John Barton, Frank Collier and Norman Cherrington.

In the Second Division

The precursor of Wigan's modern-day era of dominance was a relatively barren period for a club with such famous traditions, including a now unthinkable spell in the Second Division in 1980–81. The Central Park revival began in the early 1980s and, with the controversial Alex Murphy as coach, Wigan got back to Wembley in 1984. A year later Murphy was gone and Wigan were Wembley winners in one of the greatest finals of all time. Their inspirations were Aussie stars Brett Kenny and John Ferguson, and their captain Graeme West. He and a talented teenager called Shaun Edwards were to be key figures in the next ten years, which brought unprecedented glory to Wigan.

Edwards became the most decorated player in the game as Wigan wrapped up their six consecutive League and Cup doubles, along with a host of other major trophy wins.

Wigan reckoned the key to their surging ahead of their rivals was the influence of overseas coaches – Graham Lowe from New Zealand, followed by John Monie from Australia. Lowe was at the helm when Wigan enjoyed one of their greatest achievements, beating Australian champions Manly in 1987 to be crowned World Club Champions. They repeated that in 1991 against Penrith and, most memorably in 1994, when they beat the Brisbane Broncos on their own turf.

A new professionalism

Wigan of the 1990s brought a new era of quality and professionalism to British Rugby League. They had inspirational leaders in Ellery Hanley and Dean Bell, and produced a host of international players who became the backbone of the Great Britain team.

Wise and ambitious recruitment, alongside an ability to develop young local players to their full potential, saw Wigan's star-studded line-up include such talents as Jason Robinson, Gary Connolly, Kris Radlinski, Va'aiga Tuigamala, Henry Paul and Andy Farrell, alongside the legendary Shaun Edwards.

Name	**Wigan Warriors RLFC**
Entered League	**1895**
Colours	**Cherry and white jerseys, white shorts**
Stadium	**Central Park (Capacity 24,000)**
Head Coach	**Graeme West**

CLUB RECORDS

Highest score for	**116–0 vs. Flimby and Fothergill, 1925**
Highest score against	**3–58 at Leeds, 1972**
Most tries in a match	**10 by Martin Offiah vs. Leeds, 1992; Shaun Edwards vs. Swinton 1992**
Most goals in a match	**22 by Jim Sullivan vs. Flimby and Fothergill, 1925**
Record home attendance	**47,747 vs. St Helens, March 1959**

CLUB HONOURS

Rugby League Championship	**1908–09, 1921–22, 1925–26, 1933–34, 1945–46, 1946–47, 1949–50, 1951–52, 1959–60, 1986–87, 1989–90, 1990–91, 1991–92, 1992–93, 1993–94, 1994–95, 1995–96**
Challenge Cup	**1924, 1929, 1948, 1951, 1958, 1959, 1965, 1985, 1988, 1989, 1990, 1991, 1992, 1993, 1994, 1995**
World Club Champions	**1987, 1991, 1994**

THE CONTENDERS

In search of Super League nirvana

Super League attracts most of the media spotlight, but the traditions of Rugby League remain rock-solid in many of the towns that have given the game its lifeblood throughout this century. And the clubs in them all have ambitions to prove themselves again at the very top level. The race for a promotion place into Super League is on in earnest in 1997.

Huddersfield can claim to have the best credentials of any of the challengers – largely because of their wonderful facilities at Alfred McAlpine Stadium, but also because of the size of their spectator catchment area, the strength of the junior game in the vicinity and the significance the town holds in Rugby League folklore as the birthplace of the game.

The Giants, of course, realize that all that counts for nothing if they can't put a team on the field good enough to win the Division One Championship. They have a new coach in Steve Ferres, and have invested heavily in new players, significantly Lions tourist front-rower Neil Harmon, signed from Leeds in the kind of deal that had many Super League clubs looking on enviously.

Hull are a team who are almost being willed into Super League, such is the belief that the game needs a high profile presence in such a traditional

LOOKING TO MOVE UP ... Workington Town's Brad Nairn in possession against Paris. Can Town bounce straight back in 1997?

hot-bed as Humberside. The Airlie Birds will be joined in Division One this year by neighbours Hull K.R. Sadly for the Robins, after winning the Division Two Championship last season and with plenty of optimism on the field under coach Steve Crooks, much of their preparation has been overshadowed by the club's severe financial problems.

Cougar mania

The Keighley Cougars find themselves in the same boat as Hull K.R. – will the money worries affect the Cougars' ability to produce on the field? Daryl Powell starts as player-coach, and maybe a hungry fighter attitude might give Keighley that extra steel. They've gone so close to winning promotion in the past, can 1997 be their year?

Featherstone Rovers and Widnes are both teams who, not so many years ago, were winning Championships and Challenge Cups at Wembley. Rovers have lost stand-off Martin Pearson to Halifax, but recruited several new boys to add depth to their squad. The Chemics still hover under the financial pressures that saw the break-up of their great team, but the passion for the game in Widnes will see them grow again.

Dewsbury appear as one of the more progressive clubs of the moment, with coach Neil Kelly steadily stamping his abilities on the team. Their chief executive, Bob McDermott, brought in to mastermind the club's future in overcoming major debts, is emerging as one of the most positive forces in the game outside Super League, and he is adamant that Dewsbury have an exciting future.

And their optimism is matched by Swinton. Newly promoted from Division Two, the Lions made a big success of summer rugby and hope to continue the momentum.

Judging how wide the gap between Super League and the rest has become may well be

answered by Salford – but for Workington Town, relegated last season, the question is approached from the opposite angle.

Town coach Ross O'Reilly believes they will be among the promotion contenders, but for the moment Super League remains Cumbria-less. Workington's near neighbours, Whitehaven, expect a big Kiwi influx this year under coach Stan Martin. If the truth be known, both Workington and Whitehaven might admit that neither of them are really geared up for Super League in terms of commerce and support base – the answer for Cumbria may still lie with a combined team.

Only one team will win promotion at the end of 1997. The rewards of a Super League place will ensure that the race is passionate and intense.

CHEMICAL REACTION... Paul Gartland of Widnes knows the Chemics are determined to reach Super League status

THE SUPERSTARS

Rugby League has always put its faith in its players being able to produce the goods on the field. And the rules of the game have evolved over the years to ensure that the players can provide the most exciting, entertaining spectacle possible for the supporters.

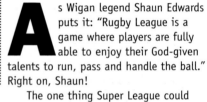

As Wigan legend Shaun Edwards puts it: "Rugby League is a game where players are fully able to enjoy their God-given talents to run, pass and handle the ball." Right on, Shaun!

The one thing Super League could guarantee, before it even started to think about its world vision and new approach to promoting the game to a wider audience, was that it would have a great product on the field. The players would ensure that – and they have.

Every weekend at Rugby League stadiums throughout the country the players provide superb entertainment – not just in Super League, but also in Divisions One and Two. At the top level of the game the elite players are among the most talented sportsmen in the world. They are the Superstars of Super League.

In 1997 every team will be looking to its heroes to entertain their fans and take them to the top. There will be a new influx of players from the Australasian Super League clubs, all aiming to make a name for themselves in Europe. But they will meet a large collection of already established Superstars when they get here.

Reigning champions, St Helens, lead the way – with skipper Bobbie Goulding, world record transfer-fee centre Paul Newlove and flying winger Anthony Sullivan among their highest-profile stars.

And just a few miles down the road at Wigan names like Henry Paul, Jason Robinson, Gary Connolly, Va'aiga Tuigamala, Shaun Edwards and Andy Farrell need no introduction.

Opposite page: SUPERSTARS ... (left to right) Martin Offiah, Va'aiga Tuigamala, Bobbie Goulding and Paul Sculthorpe
Above: DOING IT TOUGH ... Life isn't always easy, even for Superstars as Warrington's Jonathan Roper discovers

There was no bigger star in the inaugural season of Super League than Robbie Paul the charismatic young Bradford Bulls captain. Robbie will be back in '97 leading his team to even greater things.

The Superstar with the biggest question mark hanging over his head during the off-season was Iestyn Harris. On the Warrington transfer list, and still at loggerheads with the club, nobody knew what the future held for Iestyn, one of the brightest young talents to hit the game in many years.

This chapter introduces you to 30 of the leading Superstars of Super League.

Every club's fans will have their own favourites, but these are the players widely known for their particular skills, charisma, star quality ... call it what you will. You can be sure will be hitting the headlines in the 1997 season, as Super League presents its package of all-action entertainment every weekend.

JOHN BENTLEY

BLUE SOX HALIFAX R.L.F.C.

Two-code star

The arrival of Super League proved to be a boom in the career of winger John Bentley. After representing England in the 1995 Centenary World Cup in which he played three games, including the opening victory over Australia at Wembley Stadium, the man they call "Bentos" always knew he was going to thrive on the firm, dry pitches of summer rugby.

Running on the end of Halifax's swashbuckling three-quarter line, largely inspired by South Sea Island magic, Bentley had a great 1996 season. He finished as the Blue Sox's top try-scorer with 21, way ahead of anyone else, and as the Super League's second most productive runner – only Wigan's Jason Robinson totalled more yardage than Bentley throughout the '96 season. John also made a name for himself as a sideline-eye commentator for BBC's Radio Five Live.

From Cleckheaton in West Yorkshire, Bentley switched to Rugby Union in his late teens and made rapid progress in the 15-a-side game, eventually moving to Sale, from where he won England honours.

But his destiny always remained with the League code and it was no surprise when he eventually signed for Leeds. Police Constable John Bentley soon became "the flying bobby", following in the footsteps of John Atkinson down the flanks at Headingley. But it was after he moved to Thrum Hall in 1992 that his career started to achieve its full potential.

With Mark Preston he gave Halifax the most entertaining flying wing partnership in the League. John earned his first Great Britain cap against France in 1992, and he followed up with a second Test in a hard-fought 12–4 victory over the French at Carcassonne two years later.

He also represented Great Britain in the World Sevens tournaments of both 1994 and '95, and it was his suitability for the loosely-structured, modified format game that saw him recalled to the G.B. squad for the 1997 Super League World Nines, despite Bentley's playing Rugby Union for Newcastle at the time.

John had turned down selection for the 1996 Lions tour to take up the Union offer by big-spending Newcastle and admitted he thought his days in international League were behind him. But with such pace, flair and no little enthusiasm, John Bentley still has plenty to offer both Halifax and Super League.

JOHN BENTLEY ... The top try scorer for the Halifax Blue Sox in 1996 and still with much to offer Super League in 1997

"John Bentley is very enthusiastic about playing Rugby League, and he's perfectly suited to the non-stop running of Sevens or Nines football."

Andy Gregory, Great Britain coach for the 1997 Super League World Nines.

CAREER MILESTONES

1988 (Nov) Signed for Leeds after playing Rugby Union for Sale and England.

1992 (Jan) Played in 1992 Regal Trophy Final for Leeds and made Great Britain Test debut against France in Perpignan.

1992 (Aug) Signed for Halifax from Leeds.

1994 (Feb) Represented Great Britain in Coca-Cola World Sevens.

1994 (Mar) Won second Test cap against France at Carcassonne.

1995 (Feb) Played in 1995 World Sevens in Sydney.

1995 (Oct) Represented England in Centenary World Cup.

1996 (June) Ran for more yards than any other player in Super League in Halifax's victory at the London Broncos, in the process scoring the touchdown later judged "try of the season" by BSkyB.

PLAYER PROFILE

Name: John Bentley
Born: 5 September 1966, in Cleckheaton
Nationality: British
Position: Winger
Clubs: Leeds, Halifax
Honours: 2 Tests for Great Britain, 3 games for England

GRAEME BRADLEY

The Penguin experience

"Penguin has been an inspiration. Some spectators may not realize he has so much skill and toughness, but our opponents certainly know how good he is."

Brian Noble, former Great Britain captain, now on the Bulls coaching staff.

They say Rugby League is increasingly a young man's game, but nobody can deny the way Graeme Bradley seems to get better and better with every passing year.

Bradley had a massive influence on the Bradford Bulls in their highly successful inaugural Super League season. His arrival at Odsal was one of former coach Brian Smith's most inspired signings. Smith had previously given Bradley a chance to resurrect his career in his native Australia, with St George, and he went on to play a key role in taking the Dragons to consecutive Grand Finals.

Many English observers questioned the wisdom of the Bulls giving a vital import spot to Bradley when they remembered his previous spell in England with Castleford a few years earlier. The man they call "Penguin" – because of his short-stepping running style – didn't break any pots under coach Darryl Van de Velde at Castleford, and spent much of his time in the second row. He did, however, get a Wembley appearance with Cas in 1992 when they went down to the Wigan juggernaut.

But at Odsal in 1996 Graeme Bradley emerged as a vital figure at Bradford, a close link between coach Brian Smith and his less experienced playing colleagues on the field.

Bradley had a great 1996 season with the Bulls, alternating between stand-off and centre. His ability to stand up in a tackle and unload the sweetest of passes, coupled with his powerful, well-timed hits in defence, gave the Bradford midfield a steely strength and confidence. "Penguin" was the perfect foil for the more flamboyant star Robbie Paul. When Robbie was targeted by the opposition as the Bulls' key man, it would be Bradley who took command and did the damage.

That was never more apparent than in the Bulls' sensational semi-final play-off against Wigan at the end of the season in which Bradley scored a hat-trick of tries, albeit in a losing cause.

"Penguin" has yet to sample victory on the big occasion, but he brings with him the vast experience of having played in two Wembley Challenge Cup Finals and two Winfield Cup Grand Finals in Australia. He's the man the younger Bulls have learnt to look up to.

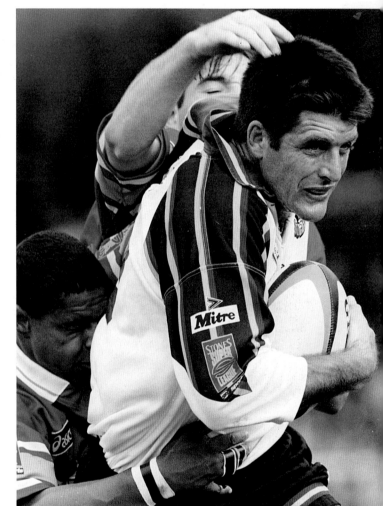

GRAEME BRADLEY... Many knowledgeable judges reckoned he was the Super League's outstanding player in 1996 as the Bulls stampeded

CAREER MILESTONES

1992 (May)	Played in Challenge Cup Final at Wembley for Castleford.
1992 (Sept)	Played in Australian Grand Final for St George.
1993 (Sept)	Played in Australian Grand Final for St George.
1995 (Dec)	Signed for Bradford Bulls.
1996 (April)	Played in Challenge Cup Final at Wembley for Bradford.
1996 (July)	Won Stones Gold Award as outstanding Super League player of the month.

PLAYER PROFILE

Name:	Graeme Bradley
Born:	20 March 1964
Nationality:	Australian
Position:	Centre, stand-off
Clubs:	Bradford Bulls, St George, Castleford

PAUL BROADBENT

Helping the Eagles soar

PAUL BROADBENT ... Looking forward to a mega season with the Eagles in 1997

E
xpect a big, big 1997 Super League season from Sheffield Eagles prop Paul Broadbent. The Eagles' new coach, Phil Larder, says he rates Broadbent as currently the number one British front-rower in the game, and sees him as the cornerstone foundation of what is sure to be a revitalized Sheffield challenge.

Paul Broadbent really came of age as an international forward of the highest calibre in 1996, winning his first Great Britain Test caps on the Lions' South Pacific tour, and losing nothing in comparison with the Kiwi pack as he

"When we got down to picking the 1996 Lions touring team it became obvious that Paul Broadbent was the most consistent British front-rower in the game."

Phil Larder, 1996 Great Britain Lions coach.

took the British challenge right into the heart of the battle in New Zealand.

The front row may be a less glamorous aspect of football in the new Super League era, but the hard work still has to be done, and men like Paul Broadbent are so important in giving their team vital forward momentum. Without it they lose the game!

Broadbent will be a ten-year veteran in 1997 – he joined the Eagles from the Castleford amateurs, Lock Lane, back in October 1987. Under the steady, guiding hand of former Eagles mentor Gary Hetherington, Broadbent progressed from honest toiler to Test star. Now with Hetherington gone to Leeds, Great Britain coach Phil Larder is the man to add the crowning glory to Broadbent's career.

Paul knew he had arrived when he was called up to the England team in February 1995. The match against France at Gateshead was marred by the withdrawals of Wigan and St Helens players involved in a Challenge Cup replay – but nothing could dampen Paul's pride as he ploughed through the mud and driving rain to dive over between the posts for a vital try in a closely fought 19–16 victory for England.

He followed up by playing for England in the Centenary World Cup, again scoring a try in his only full appearance against Fiji at Central Park, Wigan.

Answering to the nickname of "Beans", Broadbent was one of the first forwards picked for the 1996 Great Britain tour. His battles with New Zealand front-rowers Grant Young and Quentin Pongia were highlights of the Lions Test series. Although he started the tour with limited international pedigree and reputation, the Sheffield man

emerged as world-ranked player.

With that experience under his belt, expect a very self-confident and fired-up Paul Broadbent in 1997, helping the Eagles soar to new heights.

CAREER MILESTONES

1987 (Oct)	Signed for Sheffield from Lock Lane Amateurs.
1989 (May)	Played in winning Division Two Premiership Final at Old Trafford for the Eagles.
1992 (May)	Repeated Premiership Final success at Old Trafford.
1995 (Feb)	Made full debut for England against France at Gateshead.
1995 (Oct)	In England World Cup squad, played against Fiji
1996 (Sept)	Selected for Great Britain Lions touring team.
1996 (Sept)	Made Test debut in 32–30 win over Papua New Guinea, went on to play in all five Lions Tests.

PLAYER PROFILE

Name:	Paul Broadbent
Born:	24 May 1968, in Castleford
Nationality:	British
Position:	Front-row forward
Clubs:	Sheffield Eagles
Honours:	5 Tests for Great Britain, 2 games for England

PSG RUGBY LEAGUE PIERRE CHAMORIN

A French vintage

"Even when he was just a junior playing in the Army team it was obvious that Pierre Chamorin was a player with real quality and natural ability. He's also highly intelligent and very coachable."

David Ellis, Assistant Coach at Paris Saint Germain

Super League 1996 gave Pierre Chamorin the opportunity he had craved to prove himself at the top level of pro football, and the cultured Catalan took his chance with both hands.

British fans may not have realized it, but Chamorin was probably second only to Shaun Edwards in being the Super League's most decorated player in terms of participation in overseas tours and major finals. Chamorin has featured in no less than six Championship finals and three Cup Finals for his home club, St Estève. He's also been on six overseas tours with the French national team, as well as playing in England numerous times and in the 1995 World Cup.

It was a surprise when he, rather than scrum-half Patrick Entat, was named as the captain of Paris Saint Germain. The decision may have been taken to lift some pressure off Entat, but it was taken in the full knowledge that Chamorin had the strength and talent to be a key player who would lead by example.

Pierre's family is steeped in Rugby League. His father, Henri, was a three-quarter who played in Championship-winning teams with XIII Catalan and won eight caps for France, including all six Tests on their 1964 tour to Australia and New Zealand.

St Estève is the most successful French club of the past decade. Rugby League has been the vehicle for the of prosperity St Estève, a small town in the northern suburbs of Perpignan, and Chamorin has been a key figure in their success.

He starred for the French juniors as a loose-forward, and learned much under English coach David Ellis whilst doing his military service at the Bataillon de Joinville. His first Championship Final appearance came as a substitute in a controversial match against Le Pontet in 1989. A year later he partnered Didier Cabestany in the second-row as St Estève beat Carcassonne 24–23 in a thrilling Final.

Chamorin's Test debut came in 1989, as a substitute in a 16–14 loss to the Kiwis. He toured Australia in 1990, without making the Test side, but returned four years later as vice-captain, and put in a sterling performance at stand-off against Laurie Daley, despite playing in an out-classed team against the Aussies. His 20 major internationals have also included tours to New Zealand, Papua New Guinea, Fiji, Canada, Russia and Moldova.

Chamorin is no stranger to nerve-jangling moments. In three Championship Finals he's been faced with a last-minute conversion from the touchline to win or tie the game – and each time he missed!

His strength and versatility were major assets to PSG in their difficult debut season, and with that experience, Chamorin should emerge as the most influential French player in Super League in the foreseeable future.

PLAYER PROFILE

Name:	Pierre Chamorin **Nationality:** French
Position:	Centre, stand-off, loose-forward
Clubs:	Paris Saint Germain, St Estève
Honours:	20 caps for France, 6 Championship Finals, 3 Lord Derby Cup Finals

CAREER MILESTONES

1989 (Nov)	Made Test debut against New Zealand.
1990 (June)	Went on six-match tour of Australia
1991 (June)	Toured New Zealand and Papua New Guinea.
1992 (June)	Went on tour to Russia.
1992–93	Inspired St Estève to Cup and Championship double.
1993 (June)	Toured Russia and Moldova.
1994 (June)	Toured Australia, PNG and Fiji.
1995 (June)	Vice-captain of touring team to New Zealand and Canada.
1996 (Jan)	Appointed captain of Paris Saint Germain.
1996 (March)	Led PSG to victory over Sheffield in the opening game of Super League.

PIERRE CHAMORIN ...
Proved his quality in the inaugural Super League

GARY CONNOLLY

The League thoroughbred

"Gary Connolly is probably the best rugby centre-threequarter in Britain today."

Will Carling, former England Rugby Union captain and Harlequins team-mate.

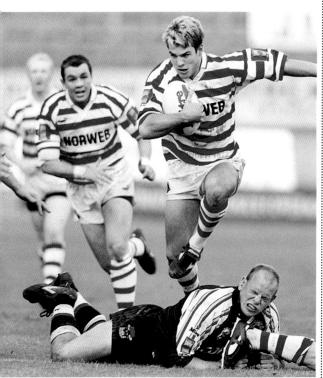

GARY CONNOLLY ... Sets off on another mazy run for Wigan against Bradford

PLAYER PROFILE

Name: Gary Connolly
Born: 22 June 1971, in St Helens
Nationality: British
Position: Centre, full-back
Clubs: Wigan, Canterbury-Bankstown, St Helens
Honours: 17 full internationals for Great Britain

Gary Connolly is the perfect example of a Rugby League thoroughbred. His skills and sheer quality give him the ability to do almost anything on the field of play, but his laid-back style makes him one of the ultimate quiet achievers.

But behind that unassuming manner and choirboy appearance, Gary Connolly packs a mighty strong power base. His defence can be awesome and he's as tough as they come – it's just that for League boys like Gary, being tough means you don't have to prove it.

Connolly learned his football at the Blackbrook Amateur Club in his home town of St Helens, and was a star for the BARLA Young Lions international team. He signed for Saints and was thrown straight in at the deep end when he played at Wembley in the 1989 Challenge Cup Final as an 18-year-old amateur. His confidence took a battering that day from Wigan, but it was only a temporary hiccup on the road to stardom for a player of Gary's ability and determination.

In the early part of his career he was a specialist full-back – the move to centre came later. He played the first of his 17 internationals for Great Britain in 1991 against Papua New Guinea, and established his reputation on the 1992 Lions tour and later in the World Cup Final at Wembley in which Great Britain went within one try of victory over Mal Meninga's Australian team.

As a youngster Gary had admired Meninga from the terraces at Knowsley Road – by 1992 he was in direct opposition to him in the battle for the Ashes, one of the toughest sporting arenas in the world. A year later Connolly convinced Australian critics of his quality when he had a highly impressive season with the Canterbury-Bankstown club. It was whilst he was in Sydney, in August 1993, that his controversial transfer to Wigan was announced.

That didn't go down well with the St

CAREER MILESTONES

1989 (May)	Played as an amateur for St Helens in Challenge Cup Final at Wembley.
1989 (July)	Played for BARLA Young Lions in Australia.
1991 (Nov)	Made Great Britain Test debut against Papua New Guinea.
1992 (June)	Toured Australia with the Lions, played in sensational second Test victory at Melbourne.
1993 (July)	Starred for Canterbury-Bankstown in Australian Rugby League.
1993 (Aug)	Signed for Wigan from St Helens.
1994 (April)	Played for Wigan in winning Challenge Cup Final at Wembley, and repeated this in 1995 (both victories over Leeds).
1995 (Oct)	Made dramatic comeback after suffering from pneumonia to play for England in World Cup Final at Wembley.

Helens fans, but Connolly himself never looked back – becoming one of the stars of Wigan's trophy-winning dynasty and confirming his position as one of Britain's top players.

His star quality put him in great demand when the Super League "war" erupted Down Under, and he was one of a handful of British players who accepted a mega offer from the Australian Rugby League. His awesome display in the 1996 Premiership Final was followed by an equally successful winter in Rugby Union with Harlequins – but he'll be back where he belongs in 1997, as one of the stars of the Super League.

MARTIN CROMPTON

The vital connection

"His importance to this team cannot be overemphasized – he's a key organizer."

Andy Goodway, Coach of the Oldham Bears.

In any football competition there are going to be all-star outfits, and there are also going to be the less glamorous clubs who pin their hopes more on 100 per cent endeavour and teamwork ahead of individual brilliance.

But in all those teams for which the work ethic is everything, there is always going to be one major cog in the wheel – the man who makes them tick. At Oldham Martin Crompton is that man who makes the vital connection.

The Bears know they have a battle to match the big guns of Super League, but with Crompton calling the shots in the middle of the field, prompting, probing and setting up his runners, they can break the tightest defences. Rather like the quarterback in American Football, Crompton controls all the plays, taking tactical decisions on the run, deciding whether to run, kick or pass long or short.

Certainly Oldham coach Andy Goodway recognizes the sheer value of Martin Crompton to his team. When reports suggested Leeds were interested in signing him during the close season, Goodway was quick to emphasize that Crompton wouldn't be going anywhere – he wasn't just a good scrum-half for Oldham, he was the very centrepoint of their whole game-plan.

At Oldham Martin has really established himself as a major player in the British game. Born and raised in amateur League in Wigan, he entered the paid ranks with Warrington and was a regular first-teamer at Wilderspool.

It seemed he had hit the big time when he was signed by his home-town club in 1992, but, whilst he gave useful service to Wigan and put in some excellent performances, playing in the same team as a legend like Shaun Edwards meant he wasn't able to take the full responsibility he thrives on as a playmaker.

A move to Oldham in October 1993 was perfect for Crompton's career development. It was a chance to prove himself a big fish in a slightly less crowded pond – and he hasn't looked back.

Martin was called into the England training squad for the 1995 World Cup, but eventually broke into international Rugby League with the Irish team who were eager to utilize his vast experience. Crompton captained Ireland in the 1995 Emerging Nations World Cup in which they beat Moldova and Morocco to finish runners-up to the Cook Islands. He also led Ireland in their 1996 international against Scotland.

1997 will be an important season for the Oldham Bears and, once again, so many of their hopes are centred around Martin Crompton.

PLAYER PROFILE

Name:	Martin Crompton
Born:	29 September 1969 in Wigan
Nationality:	British
Position:	Scrum-half
Clubs:	Oldham, Wigan, Warrington
Honours:	Irish Rugby League international

CAREER MILESTONES

1989 (June)	Played for Warrington in American Challenge Match in Milwaukee, U.S.A.
1990 (May)	Played in Challenge Cup Final at Wembley for Warrington.
1992 (July)	Signed for Wigan from Warrington.
1993 (Sept)	Signed for Oldham from Wigan.
1995 (Oct)	Captained Ireland in the Emerging Nations World Cup.
1996 (Aug)	Captained Ireland in match against Scotland.

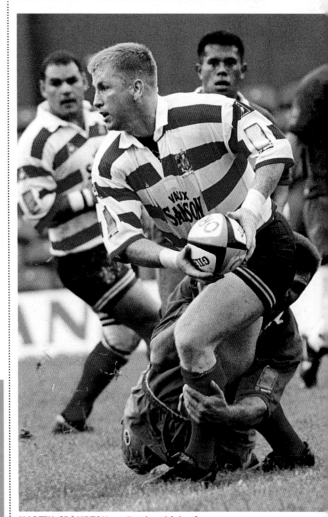

MARTIN CROMPTON ... In the thick of the action as always, he is the vital cog for the Bears attack, trying to keep the ball alive even when tackled

KEIRON CUNNINGHAM

So hard to handle

> *"Cunningham's strength is phenomenal ... he just bashes defenders out of the way and puts the Saints on a roll time and time again."*

Mike Stephenson, Sky Television commentator.

At the start of the 1996 Super League season one of the easiest predictions to make was that, by the end of it, Keiron Cunningham would be Great Britain's first-choice hooker.

For one so young – Cunningham was only 19 – it was a major achievement in a role so dominating and so central to the modern game. The hooking position demands great tactical awareness as well as quick thinking, skilful handling and tremendous physical strength and fitness.

Young Keiron possesses all those qualities and more. His speed and power-packed running from dummy-half puts him on a higher plane – made it inevitable that he would figure in the number nine jersey for Great Britain on the Lions tour.

Cunningham's running power makes him so hard to handle. Even the best defensive co-ordinators have thought they had everything worked out to keep him covered, only to find their tacklers being blasted apart by Keiron's strength and explosiveness out of the blocks. Time and again it happened throughout the 1996 season as he frequently provided the momentum for St Helens' march to the Super League Championship and Challenge Cup double.

To say Cunningham was a teenage prodigy is an understatement. He was already a familiar figure at Knowsley Road when he signed professional forms for Saints at the earliest opportunity – on the stroke of his 17th birthday. His pedigree in the game could not be better, with his elder brother Eddie a star for both St Helens and Widnes in an earlier era.

Keiron also followed big brother's example by opting to play for Wales by virtue of the grandparent ruling. That opened the way for Cunningham into the international arena. He made substitute appearances in all three of Wales' games in the 1995 World Cup, and was first-choice Welsh hooker in the 1996 European Championships.

That was the forerunner to selection for the 1996 Lions, and he played in all five Tests for Great Britain on the tour.

Keiron was voted Stones Super League Young Player of the Year in 1996, and was a major contender for the overall accolade as player of the season. Few other individuals were as inspirational as Cunningham, and his reward was the inaugural Super League title.

Now, at just 20 years of age, he stands ready to dominate the game for many years to come.

CAREER MILESTONES

1993 (Oct)	Signed for St Helens.
1995 (Oct)	Played as substitute in all three games for Wales in Centenary World Cup.
1996 (Jan)	Took man-of-the-match award in Regal Trophy Final.
1996 (April)	Played for Saints in winning Challenge Cup Final at Wembley.
1996 (June)	Played for Wales in European Championship.
1996 (Aug)	Won Super League Championship with St Helens.
1996 (Sept)	Selected for Lions tour, and made Great Britain Test debut against Papua New Guinea.

PLAYER PROFILE

Name:	Keiron Cunningham
Born:	28 October 1976 at St Helens
Nationality:	British
Position:	Hooker
Clubs:	St Helens
Honours:	5 Great Britain caps, 5 appearances for Wales

KEIRON CUNNINGHAM ... Showing he is just as strong in defence as he is in attack as he wraps up the Bulls' Bernard Dwyer, his predecessor in the Saints' hooking role

SHAUN EDWARDS

A true champion

"I'll pack it in when I see three or four scrum-halves in Super League that I think are better than me. That's what will make my mind up and it will be my opinion that counts, not someone else's."

Shaun Edwards

Shaun Edwards can safely say he's really "been there, done that". And Shaun's definitely got the T-shirt, too, to go alongside a vast collection of winners' medals and awards from a career that has known little but success since he joined Wigan back in 1983.

When Edwards signed on the dotted line for his home-town club on his 17th birthday, it seemed his destiny was cast in stone. The ensuing 13 years have shown that neither he, nor the Wigan club, would have cause to regret that highly publicized moment when the talented teenager put pen to paper.

The son of former Warrington stand-off Jackie Edwards, Shaun was destined for stardom when he emerged as an outstanding schoolboy player. He has been the one constant factor throughout the most successful era in the illustrious history of the Wigan club. In that time Shaun established a new Rugby League record for the most successful Challenge Cup Finals at Wembley with nine from ten appearances.

He also holds the record for being the youngest Cup-winning captain at Wembley, achieved when he led Wigan to victory over Halifax in the 1988 Final.

Shaun was just 18 years old when he made his Test debut for Great Britain, at full-back, against France at Headingley in 1985. He has gone on to feature in 36 full internationals for Great Britain, including the 1992 World Cup Final.

Whilst his career at club level with Wigan has been nothing short of a glittering success, Edwards has suffered several disappointments in the international arena – most notably when, after being honoured with the Great Britain captaincy for the 1994 Ashes series, he was sent off in the first Test at Wembley. A year later he was appointed England skipper for the World Cup, but after he had led his country to victory over Australia in the opening game at Wembley, injury forced him to miss the rest of the tournament.

1996 saw yet another new plateau reached in the long career of Shaun Edwards. Often under pressure for his scrum-half place from the emerging talent of Craig Murdock, Shaun rose to the challenges like a man possessed.

He captained England to a record victory over France and was inspirational in Wigan's Premiership triumph. Inspired by his Christian faith, his single-minded determination and dedication to the League game have won Shaun the respect of even his fiercest rivals. There's no doubt that, whilst Edwards has much football left in him in 1997, his qualities to constantly learn, improve and strive for excellence, will see him emerge as a talented coach one day in the future.

CAREER MILESTONES

1983 (May)	Captained England Schools.
1983 (Oct)	Signed for Wigan.
1984 (May)	Became youngest player at that time to play in a Wembley Final.
1985 (Mar)	Made Test debut for Great Britain.
1989 (Sept)	Played for Balmain in Sydney as they reached the Grand Final.
1989 (Dec)	Won Ernest Ward Trophy as Britain's outstanding international.
1995 (Oct)	Appointed England captain for World Cup.

PLAYER PROFILE

Name:	Shaun Edwards
Born:	17 October 1966
Nationality:	British
Position:	Scrum-half
Clubs:	Wigan
Honours:	36 Tests for Great Britain, Lions tour 1992 Man of Steel 1990

SHAUN EDWARDS ... Enjoyed a new lease of life with Wigan in 1996, he is a true champion

PATRICK ENTAT

PSG
RUGBY LEAGUE

Le Petit Général

PATRICK ENTAT ... Has the self-discipline of a true professional

"I've never known a player with a bigger heart than Patrick. His courage and toughness are a lesson to all his team-mates."

Tas Baitieri, former French national team coach and original manager of Paris Saint Germain

To the outside world Patrick Entat has shone as the symbol of French Rugby League over the past decade – and it was no surprise that he should automatically become the heartbeat of the Paris Saint Germain team in their first year in Super League.

Entat has been the little battler with one of the biggest hearts in the world of Rugby League. More often than not he's played in French teams physically dominated by their professional opponents but, despite the heavy defeats, Patrick always stood as the one man full of courage and determination.

He was the first French player to really make a success of playing as a pro in the British League. Recruited by then Hull coach Brian Smith after France's memorable win over Great Britain at Headingley in 1990, Entat had a great '90–91 season with the Airlie Birds, culminating in their winning the Premiership Final at Old Trafford.

Patrick's success was all down to his mental strength and personal discipline. Untypically French, he possesses that British bulldog attitude that forces him to back up and produce quality performances every week through a long, gruelling season.

Entat gave a perfect insight to his professionalism as Paris Saint Germain hit the nadir of their 1996 season, a crushing home defeat by Castleford just two days after France had played Wales in the European Championship. Patrick refused to join the popular chorus of blaming fixture overload and fatigue for the slump in PSG's performances.

"It's nothing to do with us playing too many games, it's simply because we keep dropping the ball and missing tackles," said Entat. His realism was akin to the Jack Gibson philosophy, borrowed from legendary American Football coach Vince Lombardi, that Rugby League was merely about running and tackling.

Patrick Entat grew up with Rugby League at the Avignon club, and it was fitting he should make his full international debut on his home ground at Avignon in 1986 – a 10-all draw in a World Cup qualifier with Great Britain.

Ten years later he brought the curtain down on an international career of great distinction after representing France against England at Gateshead – his 36th cap. It was a Test career in which he matched it with all the world's top scrum-halves, including Peter Sterling, Gary Freeman, Shaun Edwards, Andy Gregory, Ricky Stuart and Allan Langer.

Now Patrick is ready for one more big challenge, to make Paris Saint Germain a success in 1997.

CAREER MILESTONES

1986 (Feb)	Made Test debut for France.
1989 (May)	Starred as Avignon won Lord Derby Cup.
1990 (Apr)	Played in France's Test win over Great Britain at Leeds.
1990 (June)	Went on first tour of Australia.
1990 (Aug)	Signed for Hull.
1991 (May)	Played in winning Premiership Final for Hull.
1994 (July)	Signed for Leeds.
1995 (Oct)	Captained France in World Cup.

PLAYER PROFILE

Name: Patrick Entat
Nationality: French
Position: Scrum-half
Clubs: Paris St Germain, Avignon, Leeds, Carcassonne, Hull
Honours: 36 caps for France. France's player of the year in 1989.

ANDY FARRELL

Great Britain's leader

"Faz did everything asked of him and more, leading by example, and going through the pain barrier to play despite injuries. He's a courageous young man."

Phil Larder, 1996 Great Britain Lions coach

CAREER MILESTONES

1992 (Oct)	Signed for Wigan.
1993 (Nov)	Became youngest forward to play for Great Britain, making Test debut against New Zealand.
1993 (Apr)	Became youngest Wembley winner as Wigan beat Widnes in Challenge Cup Final.
1995 (Oct.)	Played for England in World Cup.
1996 (June)	Became youngest ever captain of England.
1996 (Sept)	Named Super League's Man of Steel.
1996 (Sept)	Became youngest ever Great Britain Lions captain.

PLAYER PROFILE

Name:	Andy Farrell
Born:	30 May 1975
Nationality:	British
Position:	Loose-forward
Clubs:	Wigan
Honours:	10 Tests for Great Britain, 5 games for England. Man of Steel 1996

ANDY FARRELL ... Lining up another shot for Wigan, his all round skills make him an awesome force

Andy Farrell has one problem on the horizon for the 1997 Super League season – just how can he improve upon 1996?

Wigan fans will quickly point out that victory in the Super League Championship or Challenge Cup would be an obvious improvement for their captain – but from a personal point of view Farrell can hardly get any better that his great 1996 season.

He was named Man of Steel as the outstanding figure in the game, and also became the youngest man to captain England in a full international before going on to be the youngest ever leader of a Great Britain Lions touring team.

And, aged just 21, Andy emerged as a captain of real quality, leading his depleted team inspirationally in a fierce three Test series in New Zealand.

A teenage prodigy and England Schools international, he learned the game at the Orrell St. James club, before signing for Wigan in October 1992 at the age of 17. Little more than a year later he became the youngest ever forward to be capped by Great Britain, making a try-scoring debut in the third Test against New Zealand at Headingley.

Farrell's power and skills, which display a maturity way beyond his tender years, made a big impression on the Great Britain coach, Malcolm Reilly, who himself had made a similarly youthful impact on Test football two decades before.

After playing in all three Tests of the 1994 Ashes series Andy was a key man in England's 1995 World Cup team. His performances were so good that he was included in the World team picked by a panel of coaches after the World Cup. He has also figured in *Open Rugby* magazine's internationally recognized World XIII in recent years.

He starred in Wigan's 1994 victory over the Brisbane Broncos to take the World Club Challenge trophy – the match that did much to promote the idea of the World Super League to be seen now in 1997.

No stranger to Wembley, Farrell became the youngest winner in a Challenge Cup Final when, at the age of 17 years 11 months, he played as a substitute for Wigan against Widnes in the 1993 Final.

Andy Farrell led from the front for both Wigan and Great Britain in 1996. Both those teams had their disappointments, but neither could fault Farrell's football or his leadership. If he gets even better in '97, he'll be truly awesome.

BOBBIE GOULDING

PLAYER PROFILE

Name: Bobbie Goulding
Born: 4 February 1972
Nationality: British
Position: Scrum-half
Clubs: St Helens, Widnes, Leeds, Wigan
Honours: 14 Tests for Great Britain. 5 games for England

CAREER MILESTONES

1990 (May) Became Great Britain's youngest ever Lions tourist.
1990 (June) Starred in Test series in New Zealand.
1991 (July) Transferred from Wigan to Leeds.
1992 (Aug) Signed for Widnes from Leeds.
1994 (July) Signed for St Helens from Widnes.
1995 (Oct) Starred for England in World Cup.
1996 (May) Captained Saints to Wembley victory.
1996 (Aug) Became first man to lift Super League title.
1996 (Sept) Went on second Lions tour.

Super League's winner

"Winning the Super League title with Saints was the greatest moment of my sporting life."

Bobbie Goulding

Bobbie Goulding was Super League's biggest winner of 1996. The key man in St Helens' often nail-biting run to the inaugural Championship, Goulding was regarded by many as the complete player – top scrum-half, master tactician, inspirational captain and superb goal-kicker.

The responsibilities of captaincy at the Saints has brought the best out of Bobbie, and allowed his talents to blossom and achieve the full potential of a career that, on numerous occasions in the past, looked as if it might be about to end up on the rocks.

A precocious teenaged talent, young Goulding was the most sought-after schoolboy player in the game of his time, and when he opted to sign for Wigan rather than any of the big Merseyside clubs he seemed set for stardom.

But problems with his discipline and his temper led to Wigan coach John Monie deciding he should be out of Central Park, and Bobbie crossed the Pennines to join Leeds. He was very popular with the Headingley fans, and for a while it seemed he was going to make it, but a falling out with coach Doug Laughton meant he was packing his kit-bag once again.

He headed back to his home-town club, Widnes, and began the career rehabilitation that was to lead him to the very top again. Sadly for the Chemics, financial problems meant all of their players had a price, even the charismatic Bobbie Goulding, and he signed for St Helens in the summer of 1994.

That move to Knowsley Road, coupled with the responsibilities of fatherhood, saw a new, more mature personality emerge, and Bobbie hasn't looked back. He led Saints to the top – he was Stones First Division Player of the Year in 1995 and inspired them to victory in the '96 Challenge Cup final at Wembley. It was Goulding's three pin-point bombs that created three tries in seven minutes for Saints as they overturned a Bradford Bulls outfit who thought they had the Cup already in their trophy room.

But taking St Helens to the inaugural European Super League title was the ultimate for Bobbie. On the way he was voted the supporters' player of the year.

Despite the sometimes bumpy road of his club career, Goulding managed to carve out an eventful international role. He became Great Britain's youngest ever Lions tourist (inheriting the mantle from the legendary Alex Murphy) when he travelled with the 1990 team to Papua New Guinea and New Zealand. He played in all five Tests on that tour, sowing the seeds of an intense rivalry with Kiwi scrum-half Gary Freeman. Controversy marred his tour to New Zealand, and it took Goulding a long time to live down his reputation as a hot-head.

Happily, at Knowsley Road in 1997, all that is behind him. Goulding is a winner, and the Saints love him.

BOBBIE GOULDING ... Regarded by many as the complete footballer the scrum-half led St Helens to the 1996 Super League and Challenge Cup double

IESTYN HARRIS

The "Welsh" wizard

"It's hard to believe he's still only 19. I wish I had had that much talent when I was his age."

Jonathan Davies, Wales World Cup captain in 1995

IESTYN HARRIS ... Has a million-pound price-tag on his head

Iestyn Harris, one of the young superstars of the British game, has created an identity crisis. Not Iestyn himself, but a large number of correspondents outside the game who believe he's a Welsh boy, snatched from the valleys of his homeland to "go north".

Nothing could be further from the truth. Harris was born and bred in Oldham, where he learned his Rugby League with the outstanding local club, St Anne's. It's just that having a Welsh father provided Iestyn not only with a name that sounds authentically from the Principality, but also with a rapid passport to stardom in international Rugby League.

Harris has emerged as the out-and-out star of the Welsh team and the man to fill the shoes of their former captain, the legendary Jonathan Davies, his former Warrington team-mate. Iestyn's performances in the 1995 World Cup, following on from Wales' victory in the European Championship that year, saw him named as Britain's international player of the year in 1995.

But he first carved a niche for himself on the international stage in 1993, when his massive sidestep created a stunning try for himself playing for the Great Britain Academy against the Junior Kiwis at Wembley. That was just three months after Iestyn had signed professional forms for Warrington after starring in the Oldham St Anne's youth teams. He represented the Academy on the wing, and that's where he was eased into first-grade football by Warrington – but since then Harris has shone at full-back, stand-off and centre.

Iestyn made his debut for Wales in the rain against Australia at Cardiff's Ninian Park in 1994. The following year's World Cup established him as an international player of real quality – his flair and elusive running could unlock the tightest defences.

When Harris again starred for Wales in the 1996 European Championship, scoring a try hat-trick in France and another stunner against England to be named player of the tournament, it seemed nothing could go wrong for the boy from Oldham. Unfortunately, it did! A well publicized falling out with Warrington left Iestyn in limbo, and talked about as League's first million-pound player when the Wolves put an initial price-tag of £1.3 million on his head.

Neither Warrington coach John Dorahy nor manager Alex Murphy, were prepared to say precisely what the problem was, just that Iestyn had played his last game for their club. Harris himself was widely linked with transfers to St Helens and Leeds, whilst there was much speculation that Welsh Rugby Union clubs were keen to acquire his services before Harris himself scrubbed the rumours by saying he wanted to stay in Rugby League.

The career in limbo was given a reprieve by his selection for the 1996 Lions touring team, and Iestyn played in all five Tests, partnering Bobbie Goulding at half-back. That fuelled the speculation of a move to St Helens, but Harris was still a Warrington player at the time of writing. Will the Wolves see the wizard back in the primrose and blue colours again in 1997?

CAREER MILESTONES

1993 (Aug)	Signed by Warrington from Oldham St Anne's.
1993 (Oct)	Played at Wembley for Great Britain Academy.
1993 (Nov)	Played for Great Britain Under-21s v. New Zealand.
1994 (Oct)	Made debut for Wales against Australia.
1995 (Oct)	Starred for Wales in World Cup and voted Britain's international player of the year.
1996 (Aug)	Transfer-listed by Warrington at world record £1.3 million.
1996 (Sept)	Went on Great Britain Lions tour to Papua New Guinea and New Zealand, playing in all 5 Tests.

PLAYER PROFILE

Name:	Iestyn Harris
Born:	25 June 1976
Nationality:	British
Position:	Centre, stand-off, full-back
Clubs:	Warrington
Honours:	5 Tests for Great Britain, and 8 games for Wales. International Player of the Year 1995

GRAHAM HOLROYD

In at the deep end

"We need experienced players to set the example and Graham Holroyd can show some of the youngsters the way."

Hugh McGahan, former Football Manager at Leeds

CAREER MILESTONES

1992 (Sept)	Signed for Leeds from Siddal.
1993 (Oct)	Played for Great Britain Academy at Wembley against Junior Kiwis.
1994 (May)	Played in Challenge Cup Final at Wembley.
1994 (July)	Toured Australia with Great Britain Academy.
1995 (Apr)	Played in Challenge Cup Final at Wembley.

If there's one club desperate for a massive improvement on their 1996 performance it has to be Leeds. With so many youngsters thrown in at the deep end last season, Graham Holroyd emerged as something of a seasoned veteran at the ripe old age of 20!

Holroyd had been a first-teamer at Headingley since the 1992–93 season, so his experience in the blue and amber appeared vast compared to most of those around him in '96. The stresses of playing in a struggling team, and being regarded as one of the most experienced members, can put enormous pressure on young players and Holroyd was no exception. Now he's confident that there's going to be a big leap forward at

Leeds in 1997, and his own reputation will receive a similar boost, back to earlier days when he was seen as one of the hottest young talents in the game.

Graham was one of a bunch of teenaged apprentices recruited to Headingley by then manager Doug Laughton. He's a product of the Siddal Amateur club in Halifax, and his early path in the pro game brought him rapidly into the spotlight.

He was substitute for Great Britain Under-21s against France in 1993, and a year later went on the G.B. Academy (Under-19s) tour of Australia. That may have been a painful learning exercise for the British youngsters, but Holroyd was one who came back firing on all cylinders

PLAYER PROFILE

Name:	Graham Holroyd
Born:	25 October 1975
Nationality:	British
Position:	Stand-off, scrum-half
Clubs:	Leeds
Honours:	Great Britain Under-21

and eager to move on up a gear.

He had already appeared at Wembley – first for the Great Britain Academy against New Zealand and then in the 1994 Challenge Cup Final for Leeds against Wigan. Graham returned with the Loiners for a rematch 12 months later, but on both occasions they were no match for the Wigan Wembley juggernaut.

Holroyd's skills make him a talented all-rounder. Adept at both stand-off and scrum-half, he has vision, good hands and a great kicking game. He's also a more than competent goal-kicker, able to put them over from the touchline.

Graham was a key member of the Leeds team that contained such well-known back-line players as Garry Schofield, Craig Innes and Kevin Iro. Now he's the one in the role of experienced leader as the newly named Rhinos go hunting for glory.

GRAHAM HOLROYD ... An upsurge in Leeds' performances will see him re-established as a major star

JAMES LOWES

The raging Bull

"James is a real League kid. He's tough and he just loves playing the game." Peter Deakin, Bulls Marketing Executive

Former Bulls coach Brian Smith has a big reputation for getting the very best out of players and helping them achieve their full potential, and his signing of James Lowes on the eve of the first Super League season proved to be an inspired move.

Lowes had a reputation for being a tough competitor but lacking in discipline. Still he was one of Leeds' leading performers, always enthusiastic and always with a massive tackle count. So it came as a huge shock to Headingley fans when they learned that James was on his way to Bradford.

At Odsal he immediately came under the influence of coach Smith. His game improved dramatically, and by the end of the season Lowes was a Great Britain Lion.

The year had started well for Lowes, with a trip to Fiji with Ireland for the World Nines. Then came the move to the Bulls and his career was on its way to new highs. Although he was cup-tied, missing Bradford's thrilling Wembley Final against St Helens, in Super League there was no holding him.

Specialist coaching from Smith tightened up the hooker's game dramatically. Suddenly, every move he made had to have a purpose, the art of dummy-half play was studied and analysed, and a new James Lowes

emerged, harnessing his physical strength and aggressiveness to maximum effect. He was at the forefront of the rampaging Bulls pack, not just a terrific tackler but a damaging and creative runner with the ball in his hands.

James had been an outstanding player for several years in the lower divisions with Hunslet, largely as a scrum-half, before a big game in the Yorkshire Cup against Leeds early in the 1991–92 season prompted Hunslet's more illustrious neighbours to tempt him north of the river. He signed for Leeds on 30 September 1992, and was promptly converted to a hooker by Loiners coach Doug Laughton.

Lowes became one of the stars of Super League, on the field with his robust excellence and off it with his personality, flair for publicity and willingness to help with promotions, fitting perfectly into the Bradford Bulls' attitude to positive thinking.

He may be living testament to the theory that, if a player has some raw potential, he needs a good coach to

straighten him out – but James Lowes has proved himself now. Although he didn't play in a Test on the Lions tour, he knows he's up there with the elite – another Hunslet product to reach the top.

JAMES LOWES ... Since joining the Bulls his performances have improved greatly

CAREER MILESTONES

1992 (Sept)	Signed for Leeds from Hunslet.
1994 (May)	Played in Challenge Cup Final for Leeds at Wembley.
1995 (Apr)	Returned to Wembley for second Challenge Cup Final.
1996 (Feb)	Represented Ireland in World Nines in Fiji.
1996 (Feb)	Signed for Bradford Bulls from Leeds.
1996 (Sept)	Made Great Britain Lions tour.

PLAYER PROFILE

Name: James Lowes
Born: 11 October 1969
Nationality: British
Position: Hooker
Clubs: Bradford, Leeds, Hunslet
Honours: Great Britain Lions tour 1996, 1 game for Ireland

TERRY MATTERSON

Broncos' link man

"His contribution to the success of this club in its foundation years was immense." Wayne Bennett, Brisbane Broncos coach

When news came, back in the summer of 1995, that Terry Matterson would be joining the London Broncos from their parent club in Brisbane, it was confirmation that the Australian club really was serious about making a success of their foray into Britain's capital city.

Loose-forward Matterson had been a member of the Brisbane Broncos since their foundation and one of their major strengths during their first six years in the Australian Premiership competition. For him to be chosen as the link between the Brisbane and London branches of the Broncos operation was quite a coup for the British game.

After all, Terry had been the man-of-the-match when the Broncos outclassed Wigan at Central Park in 1992 to become the first Aussie team to win the World Club Challenge trophy on English soil.

He'd also, alongside Broncos centre Chris Johns, become the first Queensland-based player to represent New South Wales in the State of Origin series. That he played with such distinction for the Blues against so many of his Brisbane clubmates was another indicator of the sheer professionalism and dedication to the game Terry Matterson possesses. And those were the qualities he brought to the London club as they achieved such remarkable progress in year one of Super League.

The Broncos finished fourth, clinching a play-off spot. Much of their inspiration came from skipper Terry Matterson, a loose-forward with all the traditional skills. Terry proved that the classic ways can still be effective, not least in the goal-kicking department. His old-fashioned toe-poke style may be a rarity in the modern era, but no single kick was more dramatic or had more far-reaching implications than his touchline conversion that earned the Broncos a draw against Wigan at Central Park last season.

Matterson has always been ready to take a risk. He was a solid, if unspectacular, player for Eastern Suburbs in Sydney when the opportunity arose for him to join the newly formed Brisbane Broncos back in 1988. Nobody knew how the Broncos would fare, or how a New South Welshman would fit in, having journeyed north to join all those Queenslanders. Terry had no worries – he fitted in immediately and was soon an adopted son of the Maroons – except when Origin time came around!

TERRY MATTERSON ... A guiding hand for the Broncos of Brisbane and now London

He was Brisbane's top points scorer and most consistent player throughout their early seasons. Coming to England was another chapter in the Terry Matterson adventure story – he made 12 appearances for the Broncos in the Centenary season before leading them to their great opening year in Super League.

CAREER MILESTONES

1988 (Jan)	Transferred from Easts to become one of Brisbane Broncos founder members.
1988 (Sept)	Finished debut season as Brisbane's top points scorer.
1989 (June)	Represented NSW in State of Origin.
1992 (Sept)	Won first ever Grand Final for Brisbane.
1992 (Oct)	Man of the match in World Club Challenge win at Wigan.
1993 (Sept)	Second Grand Final win with Brisbane.
1995 (July)	Came to England and joined London Broncos.
1996 (Mar)	Captained London in first Super League season.

PLAYER PROFILE

Name: Terry Matterson
Born: 4 March 1967
Nationality: Australian
Position: Loose-forward
Clubs: London Broncos, Brisbane Broncos, Eastern Suburbs
Honours: NSW representative in State of Origin

NATHAN McAVOY

The Reds' big hope

"He'll be one of Salford's stars in Super League." Andy Gregory, Reds Coach

Super League presents the ultimate challenge for any young rugby player. For Salford's teenage star Nathan McAvoy the challenge is double-edged in 1997. He has his own personal goals to reach, testing himself against the best, but what about his team? Salford, promoted as last year's Division One champions, are stepping up several levels, and they know only the tough survive at the very top.

McAvoy has the opportunity to establish himself as one of the bright new stars of the Euro Super League – but he needs Salford to hold their own to give him the platform from which to shine.

A classically built three-quarter, Nathan was marked down as a potential star from an early age at the Eccles Amateur club near Manchester. He was a BARLA Youth international before signing for Salford in February 1994. Within a year he had represented the Great Britain Under-21s against the Kangaroos at Gateshead on their 1994 tour.

Operating equally effectively at centre or wing, McAvoy quickly became a lethal finisher in the Andy Gregory-coached Salford team that led the way in Division One in the summer of 1996.

A regular in the Great Britain

Academy international team, he won his first senior honours when called up for England in their European Championship decider against Wales at Cardiff Arms Park. A solid performance that night encouraged Nathan to think he would be chosen for the Lions touring team in September, and it came as quite a shock when he missed out on selection.

His disappointment was only temporary – McAvoy was named as captain of the Great Britain Academy team who toured New Zealand simultaneously, and when injuries hit the senior Lions he was called up for duty with the big boys against the Maoris.

So, for most opposing clubs' supporters in Super League Nathan McAvoy will be a new name and a new face – one of several exciting players about to be unleashed by the Salford Reds. His style and running power will soon make a big impression. The Reds have big hopes, and one of the biggest of all is Nathan McAvoy.

PLAYER PROFILE

Name:	Nathan McAvoy
Born:	31 December 1976
Nationality:	British
Position:	Centre, winger
Clubs:	Salford Reds
Honours:	1 game for England

CAREER MILESTONES

1993 (Feb)	Played for BARLA Young Lions against France.
1994 (Feb)	Signed for Salford from Eccles Amateur club.
1994 (Nov)	Substitute for Great Britain Under-21s against Australia.
1996 (Jan)	Won Division One Centenary Championship with Salford.
1996 (June)	Capped for England against Wales.
1996 (Aug)	Won Division One Championship with Salford.
1996 (Sept)	Appointed captain of Great Britain Academy touring team to New Zealand.

NATHAN McAVOY ... Proudly lifting the Division One trophy for Salford Reds last season, now looks forward to Super League in 1997

BARRIE McDERMOTT

Rampaging Rhino

"He's the man who puts some hunger into the Leeds pack." Eddie Hemmings, Sky Sports commentator

For many years some Leeds fans have complained that their pack needed a touch of steel – an enforcer in the old Rocky Turner or Graham Eccles mould. When they signed Barrie McDermott from Wigan in September 1995, they knew they were getting one of the modern game's most notorious enforcers.

McDermott was one of coach Dean Bell's first major signings. But was big Barrie going to be a wise investment? Some doubted his temperament, his discipline and his consistency. What nobody could ever question, however, was McDermott's sheer power and the enthusiasm packed into his running that frequently provided Leeds with their forward momentum.

Barrie McDermott can be one of the biggest drawing cards in Super League, because he plays the game with the kind of bravado that sets the fans on the edge of their seats – home fans roaring their approval and opposition supporters seeing him as the big bad wolf. And McDermott thrives on that image.

Two particular games stand out in McDermott's career, both of which had a profound effect on him. The first was when he played a blinder for his home-town, Oldham, against Wigan when the Dean Bell-captained cherry and whites clinched the 1994 Championship. He made such an impression on Wigan that they promptly signed him.

The second, not long after moving to Central Park, was when the Kangaroos came to Wigan. McDermott achieved infamy with a couple of shots on Australian giant Paul Sironen that had the Aussie media screaming for his blood. It catapulted McDermott into the Great Britain team for the Ashes series, where he was portrayed by the Aussies as some kind of bogey-man. He featured in all three Tests, one in the starting line-up and two as a substitute.

A product of the Waterhead Amateur club in Oldham, McDermott's novelty value with the media is enhanced by the fact that he has a glass eye – the result of a childhood accident.

Leeds hope they will turn the corner in 1997 and in Barrie McDermott they have a powerful and charismatic forward to set the pulses racing at Headingley.

BARRIE McDERMOTT ... Busting through the Warrington defensive line on one of the power-packed charges that can make him the most-feared Rhino

PLAYER PROFILE

Name: Barrie McDermott
Born: 22 July 1972
Nationality: British
Position: Prop
Clubs: Leeds, Wigan, Oldham
Honours: 3 Tests for Great Britain

CAREER MILESTONES

1991 (Aug) Signed for Oldham from Waterhead Amateur club.
1994 (Aug) Signed for Wigan from Oldham.
1994 (Oct) Infamous clash with Paul Sironen for Wigan against Australians.
1994 (Oct) Made Test debut at Wembley in 8–4 win over Kangaroos.
1995 (Sept) Signed for Leeds from Wigan.

STEVE McNAMARA

A classic forward

"He can slip passes like the great traditional British forwards of the past were supposed to."

Brian Smith, former Bulls coach

British forwards with the classical style and ability of Steve McNamara do not come on the open market very often these days in Rugby League – and it was no surprise that Bradford, through their coach Brian Smith, should be the ones to appreciate McNamara's talents the most and pursue his signature with such determination.

After a long chase in the early part of 1996 the Bulls finally got their man, but even the most fanatical Odsal fans probably didn't realize just what a capture they had got in the young Hull skipper. Humberside born and bred, Steve was an English Schools international, playing in the junior sides at the Skirlaugh amateur club when he signed pro for Hull as a 17-year-old in 1989. The man who signed him was ... you guessed – the same Brian Smith!

At the Boulevard he learned quickly. By 1991 he was representing Great Britain Under-21s against both France and Papua New Guinea. Playing exclusively as a front-rower in those days, Steve hardly appeared to have the bulk, or the look, of a prop. But he possessed the classic ball-handling ability of an old-fashioned British forward and excellent place and field-kicking ability, too.

When Brian Smith returned to Australia to coach St. George, McNamara enjoyed a more than useful stint with the Saints at Kogorah and, as the almost total overhaul of the Bradford playing staff was put in motion by their new coach in preparation for Super League, it was no secret that McNamara was high on the Bulls' wanted list.

Steve had won the most recent of his five appearances for Great Britain Under-21s in 1993, and he followed up by winning two full Test caps, playing as a substitute in both games against France in 1993.

His international career continued to bubble nicely, despite Hull's fall from the elite of the game, and McNamara played for England in the 1995 European Championship games against Wales (as a substitute) and France.

Once at Odsal, McNamara's career shot into overdrive. First of all, he moved back from the prop position to loose-forward, where his full range of handling, running and kicking skills could be used to maximum effect.

Mac enjoyed the freedom of his attacking role with the Bulls, and his form was so outstanding it was no surprise when he was selected for the Lions touring team. Sadly, an off-field accident, which saw him sustain a badly cut hand, ruled him out of the tour – leaving Steve McNamara eager to kick off 1997 where he left off, and prove just how good he is.

STEVE McNAMARA ... Has the great ability to slip a pass around a defender

PLAYER PROFILE

Name:	Steve McNamara
Born:	18 September 1971
Nationality:	British
Position:	Prop, loose-forward
Clubs:	Bradford, Hull
Honours:	2 Tests for Great Britain, 1 game for England

CAREER MILESTONES

1988 (Apr) Played for English Schools.

1989 (June) Signed for Hull from Skirlaugh Amateur club.

1991 (Nov) Made debut for Great Britain Under-21s against Papua New Guinea.

1993 (Mar) Test debut for Great Britain against France in Carcassonne.

1995 (Feb) First full game for England against France.

1996 (May) Signed for Bradford Bulls from Hull.

1996 (Sept) Selected for Lions tour, but forced to withdraw with injury.

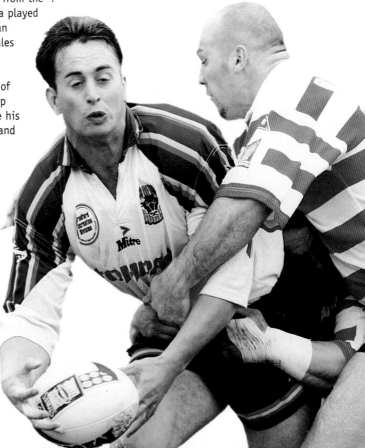

PAUL NEWLOVE

Saints' hot property

"Paying a world record fee for him proves just how much we mean business."

David Howes, Saints Chief Executive

PLAYER PROFILE

Name: Paul Newlove
Born: 10 October 1971
Nationality: British
Position: Centre
Clubs: St Helens, Bradford, Featherstone
Honours: 16 Tests for Great Britain, 1992 Lions tour

When St Helens finally signed Paul Newlove from Bradford in November 1995, they delivered him to Knowsley Road in a Securicor van. It was a nice touch, as Newlove became Rugby League's most expensive player in a deal worth £500,000.

Saints paid £250,000 in cash to Bradford, and exchanged three top players – Paul Loughlin, Sonny Nickle and Bernard Dwyer – to increase the value of the Newlove deal to its record amount, leaving both clubs to feel satisfied with a good bit of business.

Newlove soon repaid St Helens by doing exactly what they bought him for – bursting open defences with his incredible strength and pace to score a hatful of tries, many of them vital and many of them spectacular.

They helped bring the Super League title to Knowsley Road, and that was good enough for Saints as Newlove cemented his reputation at the very top level of the game.

When he first emerged as a 17-year-old with his home town, Featherstone Rovers, it was obvious that Paul Newlove was ahead of the competition. He was a boy in a grown man's body, with natural strength and athletic prowess gained without over-addiction to training.

He became Great Britain's youngest ever Test player when he played against the Kiwis in 1989, and has gone on to play in 16 full internationals for Great Britain. He also starred for England in the 1995 World Cup, scoring the winning try in the opening match at Wembley against Australia.

Peter Fox was his mentor, and he was instrumental in taking him to Odsal from Featherstone in 1993. Newlove had returned from a successful Lions tour in 1992, despite doubts cast over his willingness to travel, and was a vital figure in Great Britain's three-nil series whitewash of New Zealand in 1993.

But the arrival of Brian Smith as coach at Bradford coincided with Newlove, or his agent, expressing a desire to leave Odsal for pastures new. A long drawn out saga finally ended with that record transfer to St Helens. With the Saints he formed part of a swashbuckling three-quarter line that set Super League alight in 1996. Superstars don't come any bigger than Paul Newlove.

CAREER MILESTONES

1988 (Sept) Signed for Featherstone Rovers.
1989 (Oct) Became Great Britain's youngest ever Test player against New Zealand at Old Trafford.
1990 (Feb) Captained Great Britain Under-21s.
1993 (Aug) Signed for Bradford from Featherstone.
1995 (Oct) Played 4 games for England in World Cup, scoring 4 tries.
1995 (Nov) Became world's most expensive player when signed by St Helens in a deal worth £500,000.
1996 (May) Won Challenge Cup Final with Saints at Wembley.
1996 (Aug) Won first Super League title.

PAUL NEWLOVE ... The familiar running style of one of the game's most damaging centres, a man Saints paid a world record fee to get

MARTIN OFFIAH

The London Flyer

Martin Offiah is being seen by the London Broncos as the man to promote the game in the nation's capital city. His transfer from Wigan in early August 1996 gave the Broncos the London-born hero they had craved, and names and reputations do not come any bigger in Rugby League than Martin Offiah.

Since he entered the game as a raw youngster back in 1987, Offiah has been a try-scoring sensation. An inspired signing for Widnes by their coach, Doug Laughton, the flying winger topped the try-scoring charts in his first four seasons in Rugby League with the Chemics.

His £440,000 transfer to Wigan early in 1992, after he had sat out half a season, still stands as a world record cash-only fee, and for the ensuing four years he set the touchlines alight at Central Park.

"Chariots" Offiah – nobody actually calls him by that nickname, Martin admits, it's just a creation of the media – is a modern-day legend of Rugby League. From a brittle-looking novice

with flashing pace he developed into an awesome all-round athlete and footballer with an uncanny ability to support in the right place at the right time. Scoring tries has been Offiah's trademark.

He made his international debut for Great Britain against France in Avignon in 1988 during his first season in the game, and went on to play 30 Tests, including the 1992 World Cup Final at Wembley. He also played for England in the 1995 World Cup Final.

Martin made three Lions tours, in 1988, 1990 and 1992. His international high points came when he scored the brilliant winger's try that won the series for Great Britain in New Zealand in 1990, and scored the match-sealing touchdown when Australia were sensationally beaten in Melbourne in 1992.

Offiah now stands on the verge of new challenges with London. His international career may be over after Great Britain coach Phil Larder decided Martin "didn't have the necessary enthusiasm" for an arduous 1996 Lions tour. But the Broncos, and the whole game, see Martin Offiah as the flyer to attract new fans for Rugby League in London.

"I always said that I would never play for another British club after enjoying so much success and happy times with Wigan," said Martin. "But London's dramatic improvement and their ambition has changed my opinion."

After almost a decade at the very top, Martin Offiah faces one more challenge as the Broncos emerge as a growing force in Super League.

Even more national recognition came Martin's way when the winger was awarded the MBE in the 1997 New Year's Honours List.

MARTIN OFFIAH ... Using his pace to go around a defender on his debut for the London Broncos against Warrington

"The thing Offiah has got is natural flair – he's an entertainer. I don't think there's been anybody faster in the game of Rugby League."

Malcolm Reilly, former Great Britain coach

PLAYER PROFILE

Name:	Martin Offiah
Born:	29 December 1966
Nationality:	British
Position:	Winger
Clubs:	London Broncos, Wigan, Widnes
Honours:	30 Tests for Great Britain. Lions tours 1988, 1990, 1992. Lance Todd Trophy winner 1992, 1994. Man of Steel 1988

CAREER MILESTONES

1987 (June)   Signed for Widnes.

1988 (Jan)   Made Great Britain debut against France at Avignon.

1991 (Feb)   Established British record of five tries in a Test match.

1992 (Feb)   Signed for Wigan for world record £440,000 transfer fee.

1992 (May)   Scored 10 tries for Wigan in Premiership semi-final versus Leeds.

1996 (Aug)   Signed for London Broncos.

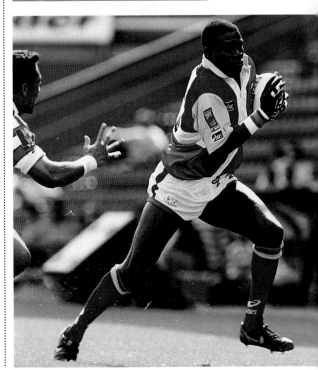

HENRY PAUL

The Kiwi genius

> *"Henry's been my brother all my life – over 20 years!"*
>
> Robbie Paul, Bradford Bulls skipper

Wigan have a long history of making shrewd signings from around the world, but rarely can they have struck a better deal than the one that saw Henry Paul's contract with the Auckland Warriors exchanged for a new deal at Central Park. British Test prop Andy Platt went to Auckland in a swap deal, and so began the amazing rise of Henry Paul.

It didn't take long for the young Kiwi genius to establish himself as one of the greatest talents in the British game. Surrounded by top players at Wigan, he gained rapidly in self-confidence.

Henry Rangi Paul (Rangi means Sky in Maori) was born in Totoroa on the North Island of New Zealand and he has played League for as long as he can remember. He first made an impression on British fans when he captained the Junior Kiwis on their 1993 European tour. It was his brilliance that inspired the young New Zealanders to a victory in their opening Test against the G.B. Academy at Wembley.

The senior Kiwis were also in Europe, and Henry Paul was called up to bolster the squad when they travelled to France. Despite more recent problems with the New Zealand Rugby League and his decision to make himself unavailable for the Kiwis in 1996 by taking up a lucrative off-season contract with Bath Rugby Union club, Henry still places great store on playing for his country.

He rates his first ever New Zealand international jersey as his most treasured possession. "We thrashed France on tour back in 1993, but the shirt is still on my wall at home."

It was Wakefield Trinity who first enticed Henry to play Rugby League in Britain, and he made a sensational impact. His greatest performance for Wakefield came in a shock victory for Trinity over Wigan at Central Park. Immediately Wigan decided they had to have this boy on their team and, although he was contracted to the Auckland Warriors, they got him.

The attraction for Henry was instant first-grade football and the kind of financial rewards a star can expect, whereas at Auckland he knew he would probably have to serve a lengthy apprenticeship in reserve grade for a team which was, in any case, only entering the A.R.L. for the summer of 1995.

While Henry has become one of the superstars of the European Super League, New Zealand still hasn't seen the best of

HENRY PAUL ... Will he become Wigan's best ever signing from New Zealand?

PLAYER PROFILE

Name: Henry Paul
Born: 10 February 1974
Nationality: New Zealander
Position: Stand-off, centre, full-back
Clubs: Wigan, Wakefield Trinity, Auckland Warriors
Honours: 8 Tests for New Zealand

CAREER MILESTONES

1993 (Aug)   Signed for Auckland Warriors.
1993 ((Oct)   Captained Junior Kiwis on European tour.
1993 (Nov)   Called up as replacement for full New Zealand team in France.
1994 (Jan)   Short-term contract with Wakefield Trinity.
1994 (Aug)   Signed for Wigan from Auckland Warriors.
1995 (June)   Substitute for Kiwis in two Tests with France, before making full Test debut against Australia on the wing!
1996 (Oct)   Took up off-season contract with Bath Rugby Union club.

one of their most talented sons. He hasn't had the opportunity to establish a meaningful role in the Kiwi Test team – his talents were woefully wasted on the wing in the 1995 series against Australia, and in the World Cup that followed he only got to play one game in his favoured stand-off position.

But followers of the British game don't lose too much sleep over that – they can get to see the skills of Henry Paul in action every week in Super League.

ROBBIE PAUL

A true artist

"There are hundreds of kids around Bradford who have got a Bulls shirt with a number one on the back. That's because they know that Robbie Paul wears that, not because they want to play full-back."

Brian Smith, former Bradford Bulls coach

When the Bradford Bulls were allocating squad numbers for the inaugural Super League season there were no doubts that Robbie Paul was going straight to number one ... with a bullet!

It was nothing to do with any secret ambitions about playing full-back, just that Robbie, the Bulls' young skipper, was instantly recognizable as their biggest attraction, a real hero with their young fans and a perfect role-model to promote the club. He was number one all right.

Robbie had followed the path of his elder brother, Henry, from New Zealand to England when he was signed up by Bradford in July 1994. But it wasn't until Brian Smith and Matthew Elliott took over the coaching reins at Odsal that young Robbie was given the opportunity to show the full range of his talents. And, as the Bradford Bulls made such massive strides, Robbie Paul emerged as one of Super League's most valuable assets.

Robbie was just a 19-year-old when the Bulls invited him to be their captain, and his self-confidence and precocious talents have seen him handle the job superbly, despite most of his team-mates being older and having more years' experience in the professional game.

Inspiring his team to the Challenge Cup Final in his first season as skipper shot Robbie to fame. And his personal performance at Wembley made him an instant superstar. Although the Bulls lost to St Helens, Robbie became the first player to score a hat-trick of tries in a Wembley Final, and he was awarded the Lance Todd Trophy as man of the match.

If that was the pinnacle of any player's career, for Robbie Paul it was just the start. Rugby League has been his life since he first took up the game as a four-year-old back in New Zealand. The other driving force in his life is art – Robbie paints and sculpts, and has very close emotional ties to his Maori roots. He was at college studying fine arts when the offer of a contract with Bradford came along, and he plans to go back to his art studies when footballing days are over.

Meanwhile, his art is his escape from the tough world of pro football. "Art is my passion, but Rugby League is my life," explains Robbie. And as the Bulls surge ahead, for their young leader "it's a case of letting the poet balance the warrior."

PLAYER PROFILE

Name:	Robbie Paul
Born:	3 February 1976
Nationality:	New Zealander
Position:	Scrum-half, stand-off, full-back
Clubs:	Bradford
Honours:	Lance Todd Trophy winner 1996

ROBBIE PAUL ... The young Bulls skipper, who had a sensational impact on the game in 1996, is a rugby wizard and a true Super League superstar

CAREER MILESTONES

1994 (July) Signed for Bradford Northern.

1995 (Sept) Appointed team captain of the Bradford Bulls.

1996 (Mar) Skippered the Bradford Bulls into the new Super League and to their first Challenge Cup Final in 21 years.

1996 (Apr) Became the youngest ever captain of a team at Wembley in a Challenge Cup Final and the first man ever to score a hat-trick of tries in a Wembley Final. Won the Lance Todd Trophy as most valuable player in the Challenge Cup Final.

1996 (Aug) Inspired the Bradford Bulls to finish third in the inaugural Super League table.

JASON ROBINSON

Billy Whizz

"He's Britain's best player by far – a real world class act."

Laurie Daley, 1994 Kangaroo star

Jason Robinson remains the most explosive runner in the Super League. His nickname of Billy Whizz, after the cartoon character who just couldn't slow down, sums up Jason – the human pin-ball.

Opposition defences have tried to pin him down, but just when it seemed they might be snuffing out Wigan's attack, up pops Robinson with an electrifying burst from dummy-half, or on a punt return, and the whole face of the game is changed.

Signed on the stroke of his 17th birthday from the famous nursery, Hunslet Parkside, Wigan beat many other top clubs to recruit the highest-rated youngster

to come out of Yorkshire in many years. In his amateur days Jason was a half-back, and he only found his way on to the wing by accident when then Wigan coach, John Monie, suggested he ease his way into gaining some first-team experience. But Robinson proved so sensational as a winger, his whole career plan was changed.

He scored two tries in his Test debut for Great Britain, against New Zealand at Wembley in 1993. Injury ruled him out of the rest of the series, but he played all three Tests against the Kangaroos a year later and was rated by the Aussies as Britain's best player. Since then he's been a regular in the *Open Rugby* World XIII.

Controversially left out of Wigan's Wembley line-up in 1994, he returned triumphantly to the Twin Towers a year later and won the Lance Todd Trophy as he ripped apart the Leeds defence with some dynamic running. Later that year he starred for England in the World Cup, scoring three tries in four games.

The sheer excitement of Jason's football made him a prime target for the Australian Rugby League

JASON ROBINSON ... A rare event as a defence stops him without bringing him to ground

when the battle with Super League was at its height. Robinson accepted a mega offer from the A.R.L. which has left a question-mark against his future in British Rugby League.

A born-again Christian, Jason is a deeply religious man, who spends much of his spare time reading the Bible. He fully appreciates his God-given talents. "I'm blessed to be in my current position. Playing Rugby may be my profession but I'm also well rewarded for something I enjoy. There are times when I do tend to take it all for granted."

CAREER MILESTONES

1991 (July)	Signed for Wigan from Hunslet Parkside amateurs.
1993 (Oct)	Made Test debut for Great Britain at Wembley against New Zealand.
1994 (Oct)	Played in all three Tests of Ashes series against Australia.
1995 (Apr)	Won Lance Todd Trophy at Wembley as Wigan beat Leeds.
1995 (Oct)	Played four games for England in World Cup, scoring 3 tries.
1996 (Sept)	Turned down chance to tour with Lions due to contract arrangement with A.R.L. Set Rugby Union world alight with performances for Bath.

PLAYER PROFILE

Name: Jason Robinson
Born: 30 July 1974
Nationality: British
Position: Winger, full-back
Clubs: Wigan
Honours: 4 Tests for Great Britain, 6 games for England. Lance Todd Trophy winner 1995

JONATHAN ROPER

The Cumbrian powerhouse

"He's one of 'my boys' from the Academy, yet he stole victory away from 'my' team tonight."

John Kear, as coach of Paris Saint Germain after Warrington had scored a lucky win last season

Warrington have done plenty of recruiting from the southern hemisphere in their build-up to the 1997 season, but expect a home-grown talent to make one of their biggest impacts on Super League this year – Jonathan Roper.

He's still only 20, but Roper has packed plenty of experience into his career, and he sure packs just as much power into his robust frame. Playing either at centre or on the wing, Jonathan is a very hard man to stop.

He's just one of several Cumbrian Amateur Rugby League products who have been recruited by Warrington – arriving at Wilderspool from the Hensingham club in Whitehaven on his 17th birthday in May 1993.

Roper was a BARLA Young Lion international at just 15 years old. A year later he went on tour to Australia with the BARLA team and impressed many respected judges with his pace and powerful running.

His second visit to Australia, in 1994, was quite a learning experience. Jonathan was a member of the Great Britain Academy team who suffered some heavy defeats against their Aussie counterparts.

Roper comes from a family steeped in Rugby League. His father, Tony, played on the wing for Workington Town, whilst his grandfather, Sol, was a Cumbrian legend at scrum-half, captaining Workington at Wembley in the 1958 Challenge Cup Final.

A knee injury spoilt Jonathan's season in the short 1995–96 Centenary Championship, restricting him to only three appearances – but he came back

with a bang at Wilderspool in Super League. So much so that he was called up for the Great Britain Lions touring team to Papua New Guinea, Fiji and New Zealand. Roper didn't get to play in a Test, but gained valuable experience.

Back to full fitness, and with that experience behind him, Jonathan Roper should be one of the stars in primrose and blue in 1997.

JONATHAN ROPER ... On the burst through the Broncos' defence

CAREER MILESTONES

1993 (Mar) Played for BARLA against France.
1993 (July) Toured Australia with BARLA Young Lions.
1993 (May) Signed for Warrington from Hensingham Amateur club.
1994 (July) Toured Australia with Great Britain Academy team.
1996 (Sept) Toured with Great Britain Lions to Papua New Guinea, Fiji and New Zealand.

PLAYER PROFILE

Name: Jonathan Roper
Born: 5 May 1976
Nationality: British
Position: Centre, winger
Clubs: Warrington
Honours: Great Britain Lions tour 1996

PAUL ROWLEY

BLUE SOX HALIFAX R.L.F.C.

PAUL ROWLEY ... Elects to pass on this occasion, but the Blue Sox hooker was one of Halifax's most penetrative runners in 1996

Lightning from Leigh

"I saw his potential at Leigh, and I knew he could do it at the very top level with Halifax."

Steve Simms, Blue Sox coach

The style of play in modern-era Rugby League has made the dummy-half the most vital man in any team – and invariably that means the hooker.

With the number of scrums fewer and farther between, and the relaxed scrum-feeding rules, many of the traditional hooking skills have all but disappeared, to be replaced by a compact, dynamic running rake with considerable pace and essential handling skills.

Paul Rowley is one of the best. Like Keiron Cunningham at St Helens, Rowley, so often in the 1996 Super League season, was the man who made the vital breakthrough for Halifax. If anything, Rowley has the edge in pace over Cunningham, and almost all his rival hookers, resulting in him becoming one of the Blue Sox most potent attacking weapons.

One of the so many talented products from the prolific amateur Rugby League nursery of Leigh, Rowley entered the professional game with his home-town club at Hilton Park. When Australian coach Steve Simms took over at Leigh, he immediately recognized the huge talent present in young Rowley.

Capped by the Great Britain Academy, Paul toured Australia in 1994, along with fellow Leigh player Scott Martin. And when Simms became head coach at Halifax, it was no surprise he should go head-hunting for talent back to his old club at Leigh. Rowley and Simon Baldwin were soon on their way over the Pennines to join their old mentor at Thrum Hall.

Another taste of international action came for Paul when he played for Great Britain Under-21s against France at Albi in 1995. But, on a day of sleet and rain in the old cathedral city where Toulouse-Lautrec was born, the British boys suffered a surprise 17–16 defeat.

In contrast, Paul Rowley enjoyed his first game at senior international level, when he played as a substitute in England's record-breaking win over France at Gateshead in June 1996. It was a major surprise when he missed out on selection for the Lions tour – so expect an even more motivated Paul Rowley lighting up the Blue Sox attack in 1997.

PLAYER PROFILE

Name: Paul Rowley
Born: 12 March 1975
Nationality: British
Position: Hooker
Clubs: Halifax, Leigh
Honours: 1 game for England, Great Britain Under-21

CAREER MILESTONES

1993 (Oct) Played for Great Britain Academy at Wembley against New Zealand.

1994 (July) Toured Australia with Great Britain Academy.

1994 (Nov) Signed for Halifax from Leigh.

1995 (Feb) Played for Great Britain Under-21s in France.

1996 (June) Made full England debut against France at Gateshead.

PAUL SCULTHORPE

So many skills

"He played like a seasoned international, he's got so much skill."

Andy Farrell, Great Britain Lions captain 1996

In recent years Warrington have taken great pride in their recruitment and development of teenaged talent. Their scouting system has been as detailed and intensive as any club in the game, dedicated to bringing the best young players to Wilderspool.

In Paul Sculthorpe Warrington got a gem. His signature was being chased by a hatful of clubs as he approached his 17th birthday – the date when players can sign professional forms.

Paul had starred for the English Schools international team and, in the same season, aged just 15, was named man of the match for the BARLA Young Lions in their match against France at Marseille. He played a second season of internationals for BARLA before signing for Warrington.

He fitted into the pro game very smoothly. With so many skills, most notably that classic ability to get a pass away in the tackle, second-rower Sculthorpe soon became one of the emerging stars of British Rugby League. The switch to the firmer grounds of summer brought the very best out of Paul and he was outstanding in 1996 as Warrington challenged for a play-off place.

Full international honours came when he was selected for England in the European Championship, and he scored a try on his debut against France. And Paul's crowning glory came when he was named in the Great Britain Lions touring team, and he played in all five Tests for the Lions on the tour.

It's hard to believe he is still only 19 years of age, Paul has packed so much international experience into his career already.

He was nominated as one of two players (the other was Bradford's Robbie Paul) to represent the European branch of the operation at Super League's launch of the World Club Championship competition, and was duly flown out to Sydney for the event.

His first taste of southern hemisphere football came when he played for England in the 1996 World Nines in Fiji. Paul was selected for Great Britain for the '97 Nines, but injury forced him to withdraw.

With so many skills in one so young, Warrington fans know they have one of the hottest properties in the game.

PAUL SCULTHORPE ... An outstanding second-rower for both Warrington and Great Britain

CAREER MILESTONES

1993 (Dec)	Man of the match for BARLA Young Lions against France.
1994 (Apr)	Captained English Schools to victory in France.
1994 (Oct)	Signed for Warrington from Waterhead Amateur Club.
1996 (June)	Made England debut in record-breaking win over France at Gateshead.
1996 (Sept)	Made Lions tour, playing in all five Tests.

PLAYER PROFILE

Name: Paul Sculthorpe
Born: 22 September 1977
Nationality: British
Position: Second-rower
Clubs: Warrington
Honours: 5 Tests for Great Britain 2 games for England

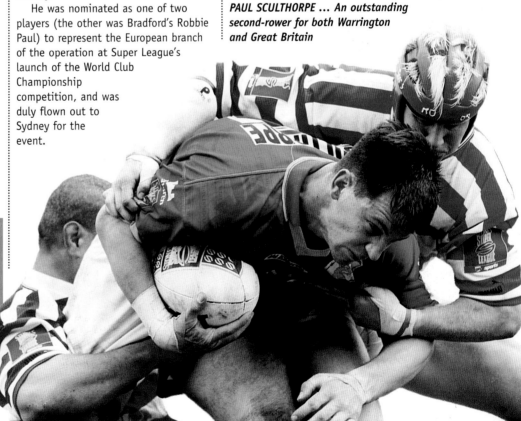

STUART SPRUCE

Solid as a rock

"He's a big asset to any team, courageous and with plenty of pace to attack."

Matthew Elliott, Bulls coach

The Bradford Bulls made some inspired signings as they turned their team around for the first season of Super League – but perhaps the best of the lot was full-back Stuart Spruce.

The Bulls had to wait to get their man. The deal that took Spruce to Odsal wasn't completed until the season was well under way, and it didn't come in time to prevent Nathan Graham's nightmare seven minutes under Bobbie

STUART SPRUCE ... An inspired signing by the Bradford Bulls, he is now the Great Britain Test full-back

Goulding's bombs at Wembley. But when it finally came, the boy from Widnes slotted straight into the Bradford team like he had been there all his life.

Spruce was solid as a rock at full-back, and brave as a lion under pressure. Yet it was his attacking play, frequently bursting into the line, that caught the eye and proved so effective.

His departure from Naughton Park was another of the inevitable casualties of the Chemics' well-publicized financial problems. Signed from Widnes Tigers back in January 1990, he gave Widnes six years' good service before his move to Bradford and Super League stardom.

Great Britain coach Phil Larder has long been an admirer of Stuart, and the

full-back really proved himself as a top-class international on the 1996 Lions tour. He played superbly against New Zealand in all three Tests. Larder had wanted Spruce in his England team for the World Cup in 1995, but injury ruled him out.

However, he was no stranger to international football even back in his earlier days at Widnes. In 1991 he was a substitute for Great Britain Under-21s against France, and then he won a full England cap in a victory over Wales at Swansea in 1992. His first full Great Britain Test cap came in 1993, against France in Carcassonne.

Stuart's bravery has, on more than one occasion, led to him taking hard knocks, as he's quite prepared to put his body on the line to win the ball or make a vital tackle. Although the season was well under way when he made his first appearance, Stuart was one of the revelations of the Super League in 1996.

CAREER MILESTONES

1990 (Jan) Signed for Widnes from Widnes Tigers Amateur club.

1992 (Dec) Made England debut against Wales at Swansea.

1993 (Mar) Made Great Britain Test debut against France at Carcassonne.

1993 (May) Played in Challenge Cup Final at Wembley for Widnes.

1996 (June) Signed for Bradford from Widnes.

1996 (Sept) Went on Great Britain Lions tour.

PLAYER PROFILE

Name: Stuart Spruce
Born: 3 January 1971
Nationality: British
Position: Full-back
Clubs: Bradford, Widnes
Honours: 6 Tests for Great Britain, 1 game for England

ANTHONY SULLIVAN

Pace of a Saint

"Playing for Wales has been one of the highlights on my career. The atmosphere at the World Cup matches was the most emotional I have ever experienced."

Anthony Sullivan

When your own father was a legend in Rugby League, it's never going to be easy for you to make your own way in the game as a young player. Comparisons are inevitable, especially when you play in the very same position on the team. But Anthony Sullivan has well and truly made it to the top in his own right.

No one could have been prouder of the achievements of his dad than Anthony Sullivan. His father, Clive, had risen from the tough streets of Cardiff, and had overcome serious illness and injury to become captain of Great Britain and an inspirational figure when they won the World Cup in 1972.

And that's one of the reasons why Anthony has felt so emotional about playing for the Welsh Rugby League team. Although he was born and raised in his father's adopted city of Hull – Clive Sullivan Way is a major road into Hull – Anthony has always felt that playing for Wales was some kind of homage to Clive. And Anthony has been welcomed in the valleys with genuine warmth – becoming a permanent fixture in the Welsh team since their revival match against Papua New Guinea in 1991.

He first made his name as a teenager with Hull Kingston Rovers, developing into a winger with incredible pace. After playing for the Robins in a memorable Division Two Premiership Final in 1990 at Old Trafford (which they lost 30–29 to Oldham after being comfortably in front) Anthony was selected for the 1990 Lions touring team. Tragically, he was injured in training in Papua New Guinea and never even got to play a game before coming home.

That was merely a minor setback in a career that really took off when he joined St Helens in April 1991. Sullivan's pace was perfect for the Saints' attacking style of play, and he's brought the house down on many occasions at Knowsley Road with sensational touchdowns.

First capped by Great Britain in 1991 against the PNG Kumuls, he had to wait until the Lions tour of 1996 to add to his Test appearances. Finally doing himself justice on a Lions tour put the icing on the cake of a memorable year for Anthony Sullivan.

ANTHONY SULLIVAN ...
Ready to use the outside swerve and the pace that thrills all Saints fans

CAREER MILESTONES

1990 (May)	Played in Division Two Premiership Final for Hull K.R.
1990 (May)	Selected for Lions tour.
1991 (Apr)	Signed for St Helens.
1991 (Oct)	Made debut for Wales.
1991 (Nov)	Made Great Britain Test debut.
1996 (May)	Won Challenge Cup Final at Wembley.
1996 (Aug)	Won Super League title and selected for Lions tour.

PLAYER PROFILE

Name: Anthony Sullivan
Born: 23 November 1968
Nationality: British
Position: Winger
Clubs: St Helens, Hull Kingston Rovers
Honours: 6 Tests for Great Britain, 12 games for Wales

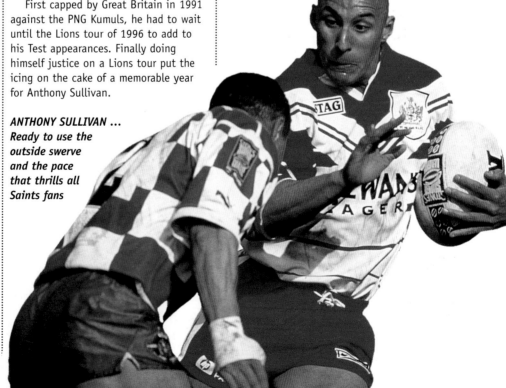

VA'AIGA TUIGAMALA

The Samoan smile

"The game provides an opportunity for me to spread the gospel by the way I conduct myself on the field."

Va'aiga Tuigamala

Va'aiga Tuigamala is one of the biggest entertainers in Super League – there is no doubt about that.

The giant Western Samoan, with the giant-sized smile, has become one of the most popular figures in Rugby League since he made his switch from the All Blacks Rugby Union side back in January 1994. 'Inga the Winger' had become a legend with the All Blacks, his face frequently featured on promotional adverts, always doing the Haka.

Yet 'Inga' isn't really a New Zealander – his homeland is Western Samoa. He was born in Faleatiu, and Samoa is the place he knows he will be heading back to one day.

"This is where my roots are," he says. "And it is also my spiritual home. I will definitely return there when my playing days are over."

It was Rugby League which gave Tuigamala the chance to represent his homeland for the first time. He declined an invitation from the New Zealand Kiwis, preferring to play for Western Samoa in the 1995 World Cup, and was an awesome member of an awesome team.

His arrival at Wigan Rugby League club, after being such a colossus in Rugby Union for the All Blacks, emphasized some of the differences between the two codes. Tuigamala himself admitted he was grossly unfit compared to the other Wigan players, and it was only after intensive training in which he lost two stones of weight that he started to make his way in Rugby League.

But then, what an impression he made! League rules gave him every opportunity to make full use of his talents – to run with the ball with such power and slip the sweetest of passes. Tuigamala won't deny that he isn't the most mistake-free player on the Wigan team, but the fans make allowances for that because they just love the sheer buzz of excitement they get when he gets the ball and winds himself up for a defence-busting charge.

Most of all, they love that smile, and the attitude Tuigamala brings to both the game of Rugby League and life in general. A devout Christian, he places great value on sporting values and fair play. "I would also like people to remember me as an example of a man making the most of the skills given to him by God," he says, always with a smile!

VA'AIGA TUIGAMALA ... A great sportsman at Wigan

PLAYER PROFILE

Name:	Va'aiga Tuigamala
Born:	4 September 1969
Nationality:	Western Samoan
Position:	Centre
Clubs:	Wigan
Honours:	2 games for Western Samoa

CAREER MILESTONES

1994 (Jan)	Signed for Wigan from New Zealand Rugby Union.
1994 (Apr)	Played in Challenge Cup Final at Wembley.
1994 (May)	In Wigan side which clinched the double.
1995 (May)	Played in Wigan double-winning team again, and then winning Premiership Final at Old Trafford.
1995 (Oct)	Represented Western Samoa in World Cup.
1996 (Sept)	Won Super League Premiership Final.

BRENDON TUUTA

The Tiger spirit

PLAYER PROFILE

Name: Brendon Tuuta
Born: 29 April 1965
Nationality: New Zealander
Position: Loose-forward
Clubs: Castleford, Perth Western Reds, Featherstone Rovers, Western Suburbs
Honours: 16 Tests for New Zealand

CAREER MILESTONES

1989 (Jan) Signed for Western Suburbs in Sydney.
1989 (July) Made Test debut for New Zealand against Australia.
1989 (Oct) Toured Europe with Kiwis.
1990 (Sept) Signed for Featherstone Rovers.
1995 (June) Guested with Perth Western Reds.
1995 (Sept) Signed for Castleford from Featherstone.

BRENDON TUUTA ... A non-stop worker for Castleford with skills to attack

"Brendon's a quiet guy, but he's the first one you'd want on your side when the going gets tough."

Mark Broadhurst, former Kiwi prop

It's become a bit of a cliché among English Rugby League club officials that they get 'better value' from recruiting New Zealanders compared with Australians. Maybe it's something to do with the winter weather in the Land of the Long White Cloud being more akin to British conditions – or, more likely, it's to do with the hungry-fighter syndrome and the chance to break into professional football.

And, of all the New Zealanders who have happily settled in England to carve out a career, few have given better value than Brendon Tuuta. A pocket dynamo,

Tuuta certainly makes up for what he lacks in size with an incredible work-rate, on attack and defence, and sheer physical toughness that is an inspiration to his colleagues when the going gets rough.

Brendon can claim, with reasonable certainty, to be the only living Chatham Islander currently playing in the Super League. The Chatham Islands are situated a few hundred miles to the east of the South Island of New Zealand. It was after his family moved to Christchurch that Tuuta first got into Rugby League, and he found himself to be a natural for the game.

Brendon discovered that, when the game is under the kind of publicity glare it gets in Australia, one incident can give a man a reputation for life, deserved or not. Playing for the Kiwis in their 1989 home series against Australia, Tuuta was

described as 'the baby-faced assassin' by the Aussie media. It was a label Brendon detested, but it stuck and, however unfair it may have been, nobody can deny that the touch of notoriety created by that nom-de-plume has consistently given Tuuta's career a publicity boost. Just don't mention it in Brendon's company!

That kind of clouded his views of Australians somewhat, and Tuuta was quite happy to leave his stint with Sydney's Western Suburbs club to sign for Featherstone Rovers in September 1990. He soon became a big favourite at Post Office Road, and for the next four years he was one of the hubs of the Rovers team. It was a big disappointment for Featherstone fans when he transferred to their local rivals at Castleford. But, with Super League on the horizon, Tuuta wanted to test himself to the limits.

AUSTRALASIAN SUPER LEAGUE CLUBS

The Thunder from Down Under

Super League's World Club Championship will see all ten of the Australasian Super League teams in action in Europe in either June or July/August. Some of the names in the Australasian Super League will be very familiar to British fans – and others will be unknown quantities, just as they are right now in Australia. The ten clubs in Super League cover a massive geographical spread – from North Queensland down through Brisbane, then Sydney and on to Canberra, across the continent to Perth and also the Tasman Sea to Auckland, New Zealand.

This guide will give British fans a glimpse of what to expect from their opponents when their own teams do battle in the World Club Championship.

The Australasian Super League is made up of eight existing clubs who broke away from the Australian Rugby League to form this new competition, alongside two brand-new teams created specifically for Super League. The new boys are the Adelaide Rams and the Hunter Mariners. Adelaide, the great city of South Australia, has always been regarded as alien territory for Rugby League, but the Rams report excellent season ticket sales and media interest in their build-up. The Hunter Mariners aim to tap into the vast enthusiasm for Rugby League in the Newcastle area of New South Wales.

The big guns of the Aussie Super League are sure to be Brisbane Broncos and the Canberra Raiders – both stacked with high-profile international players

well known for their exploits on the last Kangaroo tour to Europe in 1994.

Likewise the three Sydney representatives in Super League, Canterbury, Cronulla and Penrith, are all well known as clubs to British fans, although not so many of their players will be household names any more in the northern hemisphere – with the major exception of Cronulla's Andrew Ettingshausen.

"E.T." has been the face that has adorned much of Super League's advertising campaigns in Australia, and his impact as a superstar of the game shows little signs of diminishing. He will be a major crowd-puller when Cronulla play in England.

Penrith, who came to Liverpool to play Wigan in the World Club Challenge in 1991, will have their prodigal star, Greg Alexander, back on deck in '97. But the Canterbury Bulldogs, for so long a major power in the Australian game, will be wondering how they will fare without

their inspirational captain, Terry Lamb, who has now retired.

A considerable amount of interest in Britain will focus on New Zealand's representatives in the Aussie Super League, the Auckland Warriors. Former Wigan coach John Monie has most of the Kiwi national team at his disposal, alongside British star second-rower Denis Betts.

The Aussie Super League was scheduled to kick off on 28 February – stepping into unknown waters against the traditional ARL competition but backed by the huge media campaign of News Limited.

Their slogan has always been "the best of the best" and now, after being on hold for over a year, the superstars like Laurie Daley, Allan Langer, Ricky Stuart, Steve Renouf, Bradley Clyde and Andrew Ettingshausen have their opportunity to live up to all the hype. They have the world before them in Super League.

KIWI HUNGER ... Marc Ellis of the Warriors tests out his new strip: he should break some Aussie hearts this year

ADELAIDE RAMS

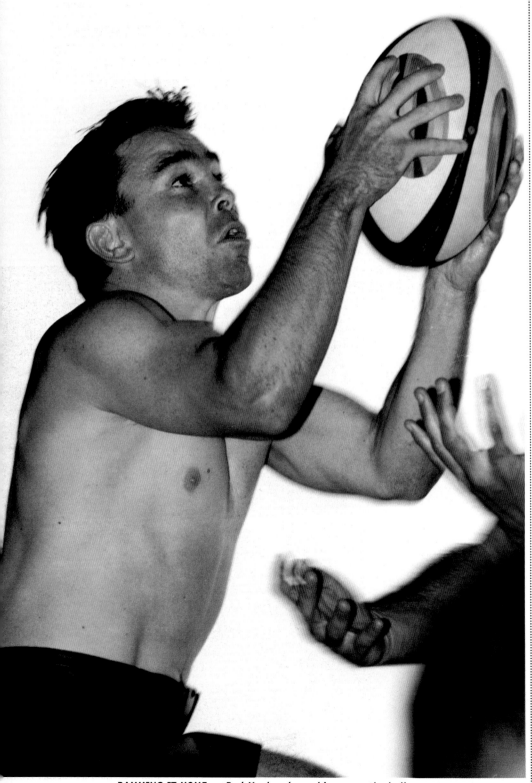

RAMMING IT HOME ... Rod Maybon keeps his eye on the ball

Adelaide Rams

Colours: Red, blue and yellow
Stadium: Adelaide Oval
Head coach: Rod Reddy

The Adelaide Rams face the toughest assignment of all the Aussie Super League clubs in 1997. Unable to sign the cream of Super League-aligned talent, they have to battle in a city where Rugby League is still viewed very much as a foreign sport.

Yet there will be no shortage of enthusiasm. More than 7,000 season tickets were bought for the 1996 season that was blocked by the courts and, astonishingly, around 2,000 people didn't hand them back for a refund when the Aussie Super League was vetoed.

Before the Rams, Adelaide people turned out in large numbers when the old Winfield Cup came to their city, notably when 28,884 packed the Adelaide Oval to see St George play Balmain in 1991.

The Rams may be too thin on the ground in terms of high-quality players to make a really successful impact in their debut season, but coach Rod Reddy, the former St George and Australia star second-rower, believes a few wins and genuine enthusiasm from his players will go a long way in establishing the sport in the city of Adelaide.

"Rocket" will pin much hope on his biggest name signing, hooker Kerrod Walters from Brisbane. He, alongside former St George full-back Rod Maybon, are the only two established first-graders recruited by Adelaide. The rest of their personnel were fringe players at other clubs, but included internationals Jason Donnelly (New Zealand), Bruce Mamando (Papua New Guinea), Joe Tamani (Fiji) and Mark Corvo (Italy), as well as respected pros like Cameron Blair and Brett Galea.

AUCKLAND WARRIORS

The Warriors are New Zealand's team and will come to England for the World Club Championship games with a massive reputation – partly because of their Wigan links through John Monie and Denis Betts and partly because British fans cannot fail to be in awe at the way Auckland keep on churning out such talent for other teams, yet still have such an impressive playing roster.

The latest crop of Auckland players now with English clubs includes Dallas Meade, "Doc" Murray, Julian O'Neill, Tony Tatupu, Richie Blackmore, Andy Platt and Nigel Vagana, and brings the total to an amazing 16 players who have left the Warriors for UK contracts in the club's first two years.

Auckland's major recruits for 1997 include full-back Matthew Ridge, the Kiwi captain, young Aussie Lee Oudenryn and mighty prop Grant Young, signed from the SQ Crushers after making his Test debut for New Zealand against Great Britain in '96.

The Warriors were a disappointment in 1996, but now the uncertainty over Super League has been solved, expect them to come back with a bang this year. As well as new boy Ridge, who actually has his own television show in New Zealand, the Warriors contain the backbone of the Kiwi national team – notably winger Sean Hoppe, halves Gene Ngamu and Stacey

Auckland Warriors	
Colours:	Blue and white, with red and green flashes
Stadium:	Ericsson Stadium
Head coach:	John Monie

Jones, hooker Syd Eru and inspirational forward Stephen Kearney.

The presence of Tea Ropati, and now with Sam Panapa on the coaching staff, ensures that British fans will see some familiar faces in 1997.

RIDGE RIDER ... Matthew Ridge may have won his battle to join Auckland from Manly, but he knows the real war is about to begin

BRISBANE BRONCOS

Brisbane Broncos

Colours: Maroon, gold and white
Stadium: ANZ Stadium
Head coach: Wayne Bennett

The Broncos were very much the instigators in the creation of Super League, and they are probably the best-known Australian club in the eyes of English fans. This is despite the fact that they are only nine years old.

Brisbane Broncos were formed in 1988 and, with the eyes of the whole state of Queensland upon them, expectations were enormous – and so were their crowds.

It took the Broncos four years to win their first Premiership, and they backed it up by winning the Grand Final again in 1993. In '92 they beat Wigan at Central Park to be crowned world club champions, but Wigan got their revenge two years later in Brisbane.

The one ever present throughout the Broncos' nine-year history has been coach Wayne Bennett. He has seen great players come and go, notably Queensland legend Wally Lewis, but for 1997 Brisbane were prepared to release men of the calibre of Michael Hancock, Willie Carne, Kerrod Walters and Alan Cann, so confident are they of their up and coming talent.

International wingers Hancock and Carne have decided to stay with the Broncos and fight for a first-grade spot, but watch out for new young stars like Darren Lockyer, John Driscoll, Shane Webcke and Tonie Carroll.

Brisbane have made the two biggest captures of Aussie Super League for 1997 in the former St George duo, Anthony Mundine and Gorden Tallis. That has made them hot favourites to win in '97.

British fans should be thrilled to see international stars like Wendell Sailor, Steve Renouf, Kevin Walters, Allan Langer and Glenn Lazarus in the Broncos' line-up.

SIZE ISN'T ALL ... Allan Langer may not be the biggest, but he's one of the best

CANBERRA RAIDERS

Canberra Raiders

Colours: Green, gold, blue and white
Stadium: Bruce Stadium
Head coach: Mal Meninga

TRICKY RICKY ... Canberra's Ricky Stuart has pin-point accuracy from hand or boot

Alongside the Broncos, Canberra Raiders start as the top tip to win Super League down-under in 1997. The Raiders have a hatful of the Australian games' biggest stars – among them Laurie Daley, Ricky Stuart, Brett Mullins and Bradley Clyde, stars of the 1994 Kangaroo touring team – plus Jason Croker, pound for pound probably the best-value footballer in Australia today.

Part of the Raiders' motivation in embracing the Super League concept was to stop such talent being picked off by rival clubs and keep their great side together.

Yet Canberra come into 1997 with a few uncertainties. First of all, they've lost their coach and mentor, Tim Sheens, now at the North Queensland Cowboys and tipped to be the first Australian National Super League team coach. With Sheens on the journey north have gone Test hooker Steve Walters and Kiwi prop John Lomax.

The Raiders have full confidence in their replacements, notably young hooker Simon Woolford who'll be taking over from Walters. But how will Mal Meninga fare in his first year of coaching?

Other stars in the Canberra side include Kiwi internationals Ruben Wiki and Quentin Pongia, and the flying Fijian, Noa Nadruku.

The Raiders' season in 1996 was marred by serious injuries to key players, notably Stuart, Clyde and Mullins. But the leadership of Daley, and the emergence of a great young second-rower called Ben Kennedy, showed there's still much to be excited about.

Canberra will be a big draw in England, with much attention focused on new coach Meninga. Last time they were in Europe they lost to Widnes at Old Trafford in the 1989 World Club Challenge, but since then the "Green Machine" has become firmly established as one of Australian's finest, and the Bruce Stadium is quite a fortress to crack.

CANTERBURY BULLDOGS

Canterbury Bulldogs

Colours: White with blue vee
Stadium: Belmore Sports Ground
Head coach: Chris Anderson

"GET OUTTA MY WAY" ... Simon Gillies is a hard man to pull down, as English players may find out this summer – but they must catch him first

The Bulldogs were Grand Final winners in 1995, but '96 turned into a huge disappointment for a club caught in the eye of the Super League storm and almost ripped apart in the process.

Now Canterbury can concentrate on football, there should be a big improvement – but 1997 is the first year any Bulldog fans can remember when Terry Lamb won't be there. Life after Lamb may be strange indeed.

Halifax fans have stronger links with Canterbury than most – with their Championship-winning coach of the mid-eighties, Chris Anderson, in charge at the Bulldogs and memories still alive of that era at Thrum Hall when Canterbury stars like Paul Langmack, Geoff Robinson and Michael Hagan joined Anderson in turning their club around.

Canterbury are still able to produce hard-head forwards who play Rugby League the old fashioned way – up and at 'em. 1997 will be no different, and British fans should make a special note of hooker Jason Hetherington and back-rowers Darren Britt and Simon Gillies. Tough boys, one and all.

And the Bulldogs are predicting big things this year of former Workington Town prop James Pickering. The legendary ex-Canterbury boss, Peter Moore, has described the big Fijian as the best front-rower in the game, and James will be eager to live up to such a high billing.

Canterbury have stuck largely with their 1996 squad, adding only Jack Elsegood, the former Manly winger, big Tongan forward Solomon Haumono and Travis Norton.

Their stars include Kiwi centre John Timu, a former All Black, full-back Rod Silva, former Kiwi goal-kicking ace Daryl Halligan and scrum-half Craig Polla-Mounter.

CRONULLA SHARKS

Cronulla Sharks

Colours: Sky blue, black, white and grey
Stadium: Shark Park
Head coach: John Lang

Cronulla go into their first year of Super League knowing they are one of the favourites to make at least third place – only Brisbane and Canberra have stronger odds. And certainly the Sharks must be the best bet from the city of Sydney to make an impression on Super League.

From the southern shires of Sydney, Cronulla have made the semi-final play-offs in each of the last two years. But after 29 seasons of hard work they still haven't won a first-grade Premiership. With less-established opposition this year, 1997 may be the best chance they'll ever get.

The irony of it is that, had Super League been mooted a few years earlier, Cronulla probably wouldn't have made it, or at best been forced to merge with neighbours St George. New administration has turned around the financial debts that bedevilled the club, and the Sharks have emerged as a solid football team under the coaching of former Test hooker Johnny Lang.

Cronulla's star, read superstar, is of course Andrew Ettingshausen, the pin-up boy of Rugby League. For members of the opposite sex it's interesting to note that their most famous fan, often seen at Sharkie games, is supermodel Elle MacPherson!

But other names in the Cronulla team will need little introduction when they play in England – especially Kiwi loose-forward Tawera Nikau, formerly with Castleford, and ex-Kangaroo forward Les Davidson, once with Warrington. Among their talented side are Kiwi winger Richie Barnett, outstanding full-back David Peachey and long-serving prop Danny Lee. Cronulla's recruitment for 1997

included Chris McKenna from Brisbane, and once of the London Broncos, alongside the powerful forward brothers Jason and Paul Stevens.

Super League needs Cronulla to be a big success in order to make an impact in Sydney.

E.T. GO HOME ...
Andrew Ettingshausen has a tendency to leave opponents uttering these words as he streaks past them to the try-line

HUNTER MARINERS

HUNTING IN PAIRS ... Kevin (left) and Tony Iro may surprise this year by sending some fancied opponents to a watery grave

No Rugby League team can have faced such a stormy battle to get to its starting line-up as the Hunter Mariners have over the past 18 months.

The club was formed as a brand-new Super League franchise when the battle for the Newcastle Knights was lost in the "war" with the ARL. It had been a long and bitter struggle for the hearts and minds of the people of Newcastle. But now the dust has settled and the teams are finally getting down to just playing football, the Mariners are finding a warmer and warmer welcome.

And the fact is the Hunter Mariners have assembled a very useful-looking team, managing to fill most positions with quality first-graders. Their coach, Graham Murray, who made his name with the Illawarra Steelers and then coached Fiji in the World Cup, has a smart knowledge of the game, is popular with the players and will have a quality supporting staff, including former players well known in England – Steve Ella, Michael Hagan and Mal Graham.

For English fans the best-known Mariners players will be the Iro brothers, Tony and Kevin. The difference between success and failure for the team may be down to their getting the best out of Kevin Iro.

But they also have exciting, high-quality players in half-back Noel Goldthorpe (ex-St George), running backs like Robbie Ross, Brad Godden and Nick Zisti, plus hard-working forwards Robbie McCormack, Paul Marquet, Troy Stone and Neil Piccinelli.

The Hunter Mariners could surprise a few people in their first season.

Hunter Mariners

Colours: Blue and yellow
Stadium: Breakers Stadium, Newcastle
Head coach: Graham Murray

NORTH QUEENSLAND COWBOYS

Since they entered the League in 1995 alongside Auckland Warriors, Perth and the Crushers, the North Queensland Cowboys have done it tough when it comes to winning football games. All that will change in 1997, you can bet on that – and the new look of the Cowboys could make them genuine dark-horses to upset some of the established favourites.

Certainly no English club can afford to take them lightly in the World Club Championships – especially at home in Townsville, where the sub-tropical climate pushes temperatures skywards even in the football season and the humidity can cause problems even for Aussies from the cooler airs of Sydney or Canberra.

The Cowboys have some of the most fantastic facilities anywhere in Rugby League at their Stocklands Stadium base – and the crowd support is phenomenal. It has been common to see attendances of over 27,000 watch the Cowboys, even when they were being flogged every week. Now, with the real prospect of success, those crowds will rocket to 30,000-plus capacity.

The Cowboys' optimism stems from the appointment of Tim Sheens as coach. The man who guided Canberra to the top is one of the top men of his trade, and likely to be Australia's first Super League national coach.

On the playing front, the fact that just seven of the 39 Cowboys who played first grade in their inaugural 1995 season have made the roster for 1997 says a lot about the clear-out which has taken place since Tim Sheens arrived.

Those who have gone as surplus to requirements and have signed for English clubs even include last year's captain, Adrian Vowles, and their players' player of the year, Steve Edmed.

The Cowboys' new blood includes proven talent like Ian Roberts, John Lomax, Steve Walters, Owen Cunningham, Jason Ferris, Jason Death and new Kiwi Test loose-forward Tyran Smith. All that, and the heat of Townsville, is going to make Stocklands a real fortress.

North Queensland Cowboys	
Colours:	Navy blue, grey, white and gold
Stadium:	Stocklands Stadium
Head coach:	Tim Sheens

TAKING THE BALL BY THE HORNS ...
Jason Death will help to keep North Queenslanders' hopes of success alive this season

PENRITH PANTHERS

Super League in 1997 gives the Penrith Panthers the chance to begin their long climb back to the top. Grand Final winners in 1991, the Panthers fell away quickly to the point where last season they often struggled to get 13 first-graders on the field and home attendances dipped to around the 5,000 mark. For a club built on such a massive area of support and Junior League, it was hard to come to terms with.

Only three players remain in 1997 from the 1991 Grand Final team – Steve Carter, Barry Walker and Greg Alexander. The return of "Brandy" Alexander after two years in Auckland immediately gives Penrith some of their old aura back. Whether Greg can reproduce his old magic remains to be seen, but his very presence at the club has rekindled much enthusiasm among the Panthers.

Penrith have some excellent players, despite their disappointing 1996 results, and British fans will be thrilled by stars like Ryan Girdler, flying winger Robbie Beckett and the Adamson brothers, Matt and Phil.

Experienced stand-off Steve Carter will captain the Panthers, who also include Kiwi internationals Jason Williams and Morvin Edwards, both no strangers to English clubs.

As well as the return of favourite son Alexander, Penrith's recruitment for 1997 includes John Cross, an outstanding second-rower who formerly captained Illawarra, and Sid Domic from Brisbane, who had a spell with the London Broncos.

It's important to Super League's hopes in Australia that the sleeping giant of Penrith can reawaken, and soon.

Penrith Panthers

Colours: Black, red, white and green
Stadium: Penrith Stadium
Head coach: Royce Simmons

MOUNTAIN MEN ... Penrith may have a mountain to climb to reach the Premiership flag, but they may have leg-power to do it

WESTERN REDS

BAD BOYS, BAD BOYS ... The Western Reds may struggle to reach the finals this year, but they will be hard to beat in Perth

It's fair to say that without a Super League competition backed by News Limited monies, there would not have been a Perth team in 1997. The Western Reds were in deep financial trouble – after a disastrous start in 1996 the Reds' support dropped by 38 per cent on the previous year, their debut in the competition.

Those figures made it clear that the Perth public will only follow winners, but whether they'll have a lot more to cheer in 1997 is open to debate. Despite a change of coach – former Canberra Raiders man Dean Lance has replaced Peter Mulholland, now the Paris Saint Germain coach – there has been little in the way of new player recruitment.

Perhaps wisely in their financial situation, the Reds have chosen to battle on with their existing troops, streamline their operation and consolidate, rather than overspend and end up back in debt.

Perth's biggest names include two of Australian Rugby League's more troubled characters, Julian O'Neill and Mark Geyer, formerly with Brisbane Broncos and Penrith respectively, both moved to Western Australia in the hope of resurrecting their careers.

The Reds also have Brett Rodwell, one-time NSW State of Origin player from Illawarra, hoping to show he has overcome knee injuries that forced his talents to be put on hold.

Perth's Rodney Howe and Matthew Fuller both have English experience, with Widnes and Wakefield Trinity respectively.

1997 is hardly likely to be a vintage year for Perth, but if they hang in and settle into Super League, vast riches could await the game in Western Australia.

Western Reds

Colours: Red, yellow, black and white
Stadium: WACA, Perth
Head coach: Dean Lance

THE TRANSFER TRAIL

An Aussie invasion

Every club in Super League will start the 1997 season with optimism. And, as always, there's been some frantic activity in the recruitment of new players in the build-up to the new campaign.

But there's something very different about most clubs' lists of new signings this year – very few inter-club transfers have taken place in which fees have changed hands between clubs. Instead, British clubs have had the luxury of being flooded with approximately 50 players from the Australasian Super League ranks who were unable to be placed with any of the 10 Super League clubs down-under.

Not all of those Aussie players managed to find a new start in Europe, but those who did look sure to help our clubs push standards up even higher.

A large proportion of the new recruits from Australasia were formerly with the North Queensland Cowboys, who have seen a massive overhaul of their playing staff by new coach Tim Sheens. British clubs, most notably Sheffield, Leeds and Castleford, have signed a number of more than useful former Cowboys.

New Sheffield Eagles coach Phil Larder is particularly happy about his ex-Cowboys, who include the very experienced prop, Steve Edmed, and Kiwi international threequarter Whetu Taewa.

With the exception of Paris Saint Germain, who have seen a massive influx of new players from Australia, along with new coach Peter Mulholland, the team to have signed most new players are Leeds Rhinos. Predictably, their new manager, Gary Hetherington, has picked some of the best bones out of the Sheffield Eagles, but they, too, have got some potential stars from down-under. Richie Blackmore, the powerful Kiwi centre, needs no introduction after his exploits at Castleford. The Rhinos also have tough Tongan international prop Martin Masella, and a very experienced hooker in Wayne Collins, plus the precociously talented former Aussie Schoolboy star Damian Gibson, who may finally fulfil all his potential. The biggest inter-club British transfer was Martin Pearson's move from Featherstone to Halifax for a £100,000 fee.

Meanwhile, the Auckland Warriors remains a breeding ground for young talent. Warrington have the trio of Nigel Vagana, Dallas Meade and Tony Tatupu providing instant quality, whilst both St Helens and Wigan have got on the Auckland gravy train, prop Julian O'Neill and full-back "Doc" Murray respectively.

Bradford Bulls had, surprisingly, been quietest of all on the transfer front during the off-season. One of their key recruits came off the field, in the shape of former Canterbury and St George full-back Mick Potter, as their new skills coach.

WIGAN's NEW MAN ... Stephen Holgate

New Faces

Some of the major recruits set for the European Super League in 1997

CASTLEFORD TIGERS

Lee St Hilaire	Huddersfield Giants
Jason Roach	Swinton Lions
Adrian Vowles	North Queensland Cowboys, Australia
Sean McVean	Balmain Tigers
Jason Lidden	Canterbury Bulldogs

HALIFAX BLUE SOX

Martin Pearson	Featherstone Rovers
Kelvin Skerrett	Wigan Warriors
Daio Powell	Wakefield Trinity
Eric Anselme	Racing Club Albi
David Bouveng	North Queensland Cowboys, Australia
Greg Clarke	South Sydney

LEEDS RHINOS

Ryan Sheridan	Sheffield Eagles
Dean Lawford	Sheffield Eagles
Anthony Farrell	Sheffield Eagles
Paul Sterling	Hunslet
Wayne Collins	South Queensland Crushers
Martin Masella	South Sydney
Richie Blackmore	Auckland Warriors and Castleford Tigers
Jamie Mathiou	North Queensland Cowboys
Damian Gibson	North Queensland Cowboys

LONDON BRONCOS

Shelton Davis	U.S.A.
Nick Mardon	Scottish Students

OLDHAM BEARS

Vince Fawcett	Workington Town
Nathan Turner	South Queensland Crushers

PARIS SAINT GERMAIN

David O'Donnell	Manly and London Broncos
Tony Priddle	St George
David Lomax	Canberra Raiders and Western Reds
Shane Vincent	Parramatta and London Broncos
Craig Mankins	Sydney Wests
Troy Bellamy	Hunter Mariners
Jason Martin	North Sydney Bears, Newcastle Knights and North Queensland Cowboys
Wayne Sing	North Queensland Cowboys
Jason Keough	Sydney Easts
Jason Eade	Western Reds
Paul Evans	Western Reds

ST HELENS

Julian O'Neill	Auckland Warriors

SALFORD REDS

Andy Platt	Auckland Warriors and Wigan
John Cartwright	Penrith Panthers
Nick Jenkins	South Wales
Gilles Gironella	XIII Catalan
Peter Maitland	Bridgend Rugby Union

SHEFFIELD EAGLES

Wayne Flynn	Wakefield Trinity
Rod Doyle	South Queensland Crushers
Willie Morgenson	North Queensland Cowboys
Steve Edmed	North Queensland Cowboys
Whetu Taewa	North Queensland Cowboys
Nick Pinkney	Keighley Cougars
Martin Wood	Keighley Cougars

WARRINGTON WOLVES

Nigel Vagana	Auckland Warriors
Dallas Meade	Auckland Warriors
Tony Tatupu	Auckland Warriors

WIGAN WARRIORS

Stephen Holgate	Workington Town
Ian Sherratt	Oldham Bears
David "Doc" Murray	Auckland Warriors

STONES SUPER LEAGUE PLAYER RATINGS

Who were the form players of Super League in 1996? Every month throughout the season the Stones Super League Ratings were presented exclusively in Open Rugby magazine, in which the top five players in each position on the field were chosen. The Ratings, supported by Stones, sponsors of the Super League, were chosen by Open Rugby correspondents, based on players' performances in the previous month.

Only one man got the perfect five – that is, top rating in all five months of the season – Wigan and Great Britain captain Andy Farrell (pictured left), who totally dominated the loose-forward ratings.

Hot on the heels of Farrell were his Wigan team-mates Va'aiga Tuigamala, Jason Robinson and Henry Paul, plus Bradford's Robbie Paul and Warrington's Paul Sculthorpe, who found his votes split between second-row and loose-forward positions.

The Stones Super League Ratings were a topic for discussion throughout the season, and the 1997 Ratings will be eagerly awaited in *Open Rugby*.

Stones Form Team for the 1996 Season

(Based on the monthly form ratings votes)

Full-back
Kris Radlinski
(Wigan)

Winger
Jason Robinson
(Wigan)

Centre
Va'aiga Tuigamala
(Wigan)

Centre
Paul Newlove
(St Helens)

Winger
John Bentley
(Halifax)

Stand-off
Henry Paul
(Wigan)

Scrum-half
Robbie Paul
(Bradford)

Front-rower
Terry O'Connor
(Wigan)

Hooker
Keiron Cunningham
(St Helens)

Front-rower
Apollo Perelini
(St Helens)

Second-rower
Bernard Dwyer
(Bradford)

Second-rower
Paul Sculthorpe
(Warrington)

Loose-forward
Andy Farrell
(Wigan)

Top Ten Players of 1996

Overall

		Votes
1	Andy Farrell (Wigan)	25
2	Va'aiga Tuigamala (Wigan)	23
3	Jason Robinson (Wigan)	22
	Henry Paul (Wigan)	22
	Paul Sculthorpe (Warrington)	22
6	Robbie Paul (Bradford)	21
7	Keiron Cunningham (St Helens)	20
8	Bobbie Goulding (St Helens)	19
9	Paul Rowley (Halifax)	17
10	Terry O'Connor (Wigan)	16

Full-backs

		Votes
1	Kris Radlinski (Wigan)	14
2	Stuart Spruce (Bradford)	13
3	Steve Prescott (St Helens)	10
4	Greg Barwick (London)	9
5	Paul Atcheson (Oldham)	8
6	Dion Bird (Paris)	6
7	Jason Flowers (Castleford)	5
8	Anthony Gibbons (Leeds)	3
9	Mike Umaga (Halifax)	2
10	Duncan McRae (London)	1
	Marcus St Hilaire (Leeds)	1
	Graham Steadman (Castleford)	1

Wingers

		Votes
1	Jason Robinson (Wigan)	22
2	John Bentley (Halifax)	8
3	Chris Smith (Castleford)	7
4	Mark Forster (Warrington)	6
5	Danny Arnold (St Helens)	5
6	Pascal Bomati (Paris)	4
	Anthony Sullivan (St Helens)	4
	Martin Offiah (*Wigan)	4
	Richard Henare (Warrington)	4
7	Scott Roskell (London)	3
	Lynton Stott (Sheffield)	3
8	Jon Scales (Bradford)	2
9	Keith Senior (Sheffield)	1
	John Minto (London)	1
	Joey Hayes (St Helens)	1

*Offiah later transferred to the London Broncos

Centres

		Votes
1	Va'aiga Tuigamala (Wigan)	23
2	Paul Newlove (St Helens)	12
3	Gary Connolly (Wigan)	8
4	Matt Calland (Bradford)	7
5	Pierre Chamorin (Paris)	6
6	Toa Kohe-Love (Warrington)	4
	Jonathan Roper (Warrington)	4
7	Greg Barwick (London)	3
8	Kieren Meyer (London)	2
	John Schuster (Halifax)	2
	Asa Amone (Halifax)	2
9	Jean-Marc Garcia (Sheffield)	1
	Alan Hunte (St Helens)	1

Stand-offs

		Votes
1	Henry Paul (Wigan)	22
2	Graeme Bradley (Bradford)	10
	Iestyn Harris (Warrington)	10
3	Frano Botica (Castleford)	9
4	Tulsen Tollett (London)	5
	Duncan MacRae (London)	5
5	Tommy Martyn (St Helens)	4
	Karle Hammond (St Helens)	4
6	Francis Maloney (Oldham)	3
7	Ryan Sheridan (Sheffield)	2
8	Tony Kemp (Leeds)	1

Scrum-halves

		Votes
1	Robbie Paul (Bradford)	21
2	Bobbie Goulding (St Helens)	19
3	Shaun Edwards (Wigan)	13
4	Patrick Entat (Paris)	8
5	Tony Smith (Castleford)	6
6	Graham Holroyd (Leeds)	4
7	Martin Crompton (Oldham)	2
8	Craig Dean (Halifax)	1
	Mark Aston (Sheffield)	1

Front-rowers

		Votes
1	Terry O'Connor (Wigan)	16
2	Apollo Perelini (St Helens)	14
3	Tony Mestrov (London)	10
	Brian McDermott (Bradford)	10
4	Paul Broadbent (Sheffield)	5
	Karl Harrison (Halifax)	5
5	Karl Fairbank (Bradford)	4
6	Mark Hilton (Warrington)	2
	Ian Pickavance (St Helens)	2
7	Barrie McDermott (Leeds)	1
	Rowland Phillips (Workington)	1
	Gregory Kacala (Paris)	1

Hookers

		Votes
1	Keiron Cunningham (St Helens)	20
2	Paul Rowley (Halifax)	17
3	James Lowes (Bradford)	14
4	Martin Hall (Wigan)	10
5	Johnny Lawless (Sheffield)	7
6	Tony Rea (London)	3
7	Mick Shaw (Leeds)	2
	Richard Russell (Castleford)	2

Second-rowers

		Votes
1	Bernard Dwyer (Bradford)	11
2	Paul Sculthorpe (Warrington)	10
3	Derek McVey (St Helens)	8
4	Chris Joynt (St Helens)	7
	Jeremy Donougher (Bradford)	7
5	Peter Gill (London)	5
6	Mick Cassidy (Wigan)	4
	Darren Adams (Paris)	4
7	Carl Gillespie (Halifax)	3
8	Andrew Schick (Castleford)	2
	Stephen Holgate (Workington)	2
	Jacques Pech (Paris)	2
9	Ian Knott (Warrington)	1
	Rowland Phillips (Workington)	1
	Vila Matautia (St Helens)	1
	Steve Rosolen (London)	1
	Paul Medley (Bradford)	1

ROBBIE PAUL ... Top scrum-half

Loose-forwards

		Votes
1	Andy Farrell (Wigan)	25
2	Paul Sculthorpe (Warrington)	12
3	Steve McNamara (Bradford)	9
4	Peter Gill (London)	8
5	Terry Matterson (London)	6
6	Jacques Pech (Paris)	4
	Brendon Tuuta (Castleford)	4
	David Bradbury (Oldham)	4
7	Karle Hammond (St Helens)	2
	Martin Moana (Halifax)	2
	Chris Joynt (St Helens)	2
8	Howard Hill (Oldham)	1
	Vea Bloomfield (Paris)	1

SUPER LEAGUE RECORDS

The first Super League season produced an extravaganza of scoring, and all the outstanding feats of the campaign are highlighted here. The statistics given refer only to Super League matches and do not include Cup-ties or Premiership matches.

TOP TEN TRIES

1	Paul Newlove (St Helens)	28
2	Jason Robinson (Wigan)	24
3	John Bentley (Halifax)	21
4	Henry Paul (Wigan)	20
5	Danny Arnold (St Helens)	19
6	Robbie Paul (Bradford)	18
7	Richard Henare (Warrington)	17
	Keith Senior (Sheffield)	17
9	Greg Barwick (London)	16
	Rob Smyth (Wigan)	16
	Anthony Sullivan (St Helens)	16

TOP TEN GOALS

1	Bobbie Goulding (St Helens)	(3)	120
2	Andrew Farrell (Wigan)		103
	John Schuster (Halifax)	(2)	103
4	Mark Aston (Sheffield)	(1)	87
5	Frano Botica (Castleford)	(2)	86
6	Steve McNamara (Bradford)	(2)	80
7	Graham Holroyd (Leeds)	(2)	78
8	Iestyn Harris (Warrington)	(2)	65
9	Greg Barwick (London)	(2)	52
10	Francis Maloney (Oldham)		45

Note: Drop goals included in total

DROP GOALS

No player scored five or more

TOP TEN POINTS

		T	G	DG	Pts
1	Bobbie Goulding (St Helens)	5	117	3	257
2	John Schuster (Halifax)	8	101	2	236
3	Andrew Farrell (Wigan)	5	103	0	226
4	Graham Holroyd (Leeds)	11	76	2	198
5	Frano Botica (Castleford)	5	84	2	190
6	Mark Aston (Sheffield)	2	86	1	181
7	Greg Barwick (London)	16	50	2	166
8	Steve McNamara (Bradford)	1	78	2	162
9	Iestyn Harris (Warrington)	4	63	2	144
10	Francis Maloney (Oldham)	6	45	0	114

PLAYERS' MATCH RECORDS

Most tries: 5 Mike Umaga (Halifax) v Workington; Jason Robinson (Wigan) v Leeds

Most goals: 11 Terry Matterson (London) v Workington; Bobbie Goulding (St Helens) v Castleford; John Schuster (Halifax) v Workington

Most points: 28 (6g, 4t) Greg Barwick (London) v Castleford

PLAYERS' SEASON RECORDS

Most tries: 28 Paul Newlove (St Helens)

Most goals: 120 Bobbie Goulding (St Helens)

Most points: 257 (5t, 117g, 3dg) Bobbie Goulding (St Helens)

TEAM RECORDS

Highest score and widest margin:	Wigan 78, Workington 4
Highest away score:	Workington 16, Wigan 64
Widest away win margin:	Workington 0, St Helens 62
Lowest winning score:	Workington 14, Paris 10
Highest points aggregate:	96 (Leeds 68, Workington 28)
Lowest points aggregate:	21 (Warrington 0, Wigan 21)
Most points by losing team:	Bradford 60, Paris 32; Sheffield 32, St Helens 43 (at Cardiff RU)
Highest score draw:	Paris 24, Oldham 24
Longest winning run and best opening sequence:	12 by St Helens
Longest unbeaten run:	13 (including a draw) by Wigan
Longest losing run and run without a win:	11 by Paris
Longest opening run of defeats:	5 by Halifax and Workington
Longest opening run without a win:	8 (including a draw) by Workington
Biggest attendance:	20,429 Wigan v St Helens
Lowest attendance:	1,400 Workington vs. London

OUTSTANDING SCORING FEATS (PLAYERS)

Five tries or more in a match: 5 Mike Umaga (Halifax) v Workington
Jason Robinson (Wigan) v Leeds

Ten goals or more in a match: 11 Terry Matterson (London) v
Workington;
Bobbie Goulding (St Helens) v
Castleford;
John Schuster (Halifax) v
Workington;
10 Bobbie Goulding (St Helens) v
Sheffield;
Graham Holroyd (Leeds) v
Workington;
John Schuster (Halifax) v Leeds

25 points or more in a match: 28 Greg Barwick (London) v Castleford;
26 Terry Matterson (London) v
Workington T.

TOP TEN BIGGEST SCORES (TEAMS)

Home

1	Wigan	78	4	Workington
2	Wigan	76	8	Paris
3	Halifax	74	14	Workington
4	Leeds	68	28	Workington
5	St Helens	68	2	Sheffield
6	Wigan	68	14	Leeds
7	St Helens	66	18	Oldham
8	St Helens	66	14	Warrington
9	Bradford	64	22	Sheffield
10	Halifax	64	24	Leeds

Away

1	Workington	16	64	Wigan
2	Workington	0	62	St Helens
3	Oldham	16	56	Wigan
4	Leeds	18	56	Bradford
5	Workington	22	54	Sheffield
6	Oldham	18	54	St Helens
7	Sheffield	12	54	Wigan
8	Paris	22	54	Castleford
9	London	24	52	Halifax
10	Halifax	4	50	Wigan

JOHN SCHUSTER ... Halifax's Samoan centre was Super League's second-highest points scorer in 1996

ATTENDANCES (HOME LEAGUE MATCHES)

		Total	Average
1	Bradford	113,809	10,346
2	St Helens	112,427	10,221
3	Wigan	111,850	10,168
4	Leeds	94,395	8,581
5	Paris	88,289	8,026
6	London	62,693	5,698
7	Halifax	55,912	5,083
8	Warrington	56,724	5,157
9	Castleford	55,137	5,012
10	Sheffield	50,747	4,613
11	Oldham	39,914	3,629
12	Workington	25,538	2,322

TOP TEN CROWDS

1	20,429	Wigan v St Helens
2	18,098	St Helens v Warrington
3	17,873	Paris v Sheffield
4	17,360	Bradford v Wigan
5	15,883	St Helens v Wigan
6	15,107	Paris v Leeds
7	14,620	Wigan v Warrington
8	13,196	Bradford v Halifax
9	11,848	Leeds v St Helens
10	11,467	Bradford v St Helens

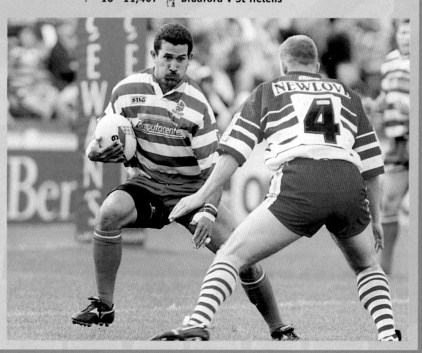

1997 SUPER LEAGUE

Friday, 14 March 1997
Bradford Bulls v Warrington Wolves (7:30 BSkyB) ..... – .....

Sunday, 16 March 1997
Leeds Rhinos v Oldham Bears (3:00) ..... – .....
London Broncos v St Helens (6:35 BSkyB) ..... – .....
Salford Reds v Castleford Tigers (3:00) ..... – .....
Sheffield Eagles v Paris St Germain (3:15) ..... – .....
Wigan Warriors v Halifax Blue Sox (3:00) ..... – .....

Friday, 21 March 1997
Paris St Germain v Leeds Rhinos (8:00) ..... – .....
Warrington Wolves v London Broncos (7:30 BSkyB) ..... – .....

Sunday, 23 March 1997
Castleford Tigers v Wigan Warriors (6:35 BSkyB) ..... – .....
Halifax Blue Sox v Sheffield Eagles (3:00) ..... – .....
Oldham Bears v Bradford Bulls (3:00) ..... – .....
St Helens v Salford Reds (3:00) ..... – .....

Friday, 28 March 1997
Bradford Bulls v Halifax Blue Sox (7:30) ..... – .....
Leeds Rhinos v Castleford Tigers (7:30) ..... – .....
London Broncos v Paris St Germain (3:00) ..... – .....
Salford Reds v Oldham Bears (3:00) ..... – .....
Sheffield Eagles v Warrington Wolves (7:30) ..... – .....
Wigan Warriors v St Helens (5:00 BSkyB) ..... – .....

Monday, 31 March 1997 (Easter Monday)
Castleford Tigers v Bradford Bulls (2:30 BSkyB) ..... – .....
Halifax Blue Sox v Leeds Rhinos (3:00) ..... – .....
Salford Reds v Paris St Germain (3:00) ..... – .....
St Helens v Sheffield Eagles (3:00) ..... – .....
Warrington Wolves v Wigan Warriors (3:00) ..... – .....

Tuesday, 1 April 1997
Oldham Bears v London Broncos (7:30) ..... – .....

Friday, 4 April 1997
Leeds Rhinos v Wigan Warriors (7:30 BSkyB) ..... – .....

Saturday, 5 April 1997
Paris St Germain v St Helens (8:00) ..... – .....

Sunday, 6 April 1997
Bradford Bulls v London Broncos (6:00) ..... – .....
Halifax Blue Sox v Salford Reds (3:00) ..... – .....
Sheffield Eagles v Castleford Tigers (6:35 BSkyB) ..... – .....
Warrington Wolves v Oldham Bears (3:00) ..... – .....

Friday, 11 April 1997
Leeds Rhinos v St Helens (7:30) ..... – .....
Salford Reds v Sheffield Eagles (7:30) ..... – .....
Wigan Warriors v Bradford Bulls (7:30 BSkyB) ..... – .....

Sunday, 13 April 1997
Castleford Tigers v Warrington Wolves (3:30) ..... – .....
Halifax Blue Sox v London Broncos (3:00) ..... – .....
Oldham Bears v Paris St Germain – 6:35 (BSkyB) ..... – .....

Friday, 18 April 1997
Paris St Germain v Bradford Bulls (8:30 BSkyB) ..... – .....

Saturday, 19 April 1997
London Broncos v Salford Reds (3:00) ..... – .....

Sunday, 20 April 1997
Castleford Tigers v Halifax Blue Sox (3:30) ..... – .....
Sheffield Eagles v Leeds Rhinos (6:35 BSkyB) ..... – .....
St Helens v Warrington Wolves (3:00) ..... – .....
Wigan Warriors v Oldham Bears (3:00) ..... – .....

Friday, 25 April 1997
Salford Reds v Wigan Warriors (7:30 BSkyB) ..... – .....

Sunday, 27 April 1997
Bradford Bulls v Sheffield Eagles (6:00) ..... – .....
London Broncos v Leeds Rhinos (6:35 BSkyB) ..... – .....
Oldham Bears v Halifax Blue Sox (3:00) ..... – .....
St Helens v Castleford Tigers (3:00) @ Anfield ..... – .....
Warrington Wolves v Paris St Germain (3:00) ..... – .....

Monday, 5 May 1997
Leeds Rhinos v Paris St Germain (7:30) ..... – .....

Friday, 9 May 1997
Wigan Warriors v London Broncos (7:30 BSkyB) ..... – .....

Sunday, 11 May 1997
Bradford Bulls v St Helens (7:30 BSkyB) ..... – .....
Castleford Tigers v Paris St Germain (3:30) ..... – .....
Halifax Blue Sox v Warrington Wolves (3:00) ..... – .....
Salford Reds v Leeds Rhinos (3:00) ..... – .....
Sheffield Eagles v Oldham Bears (3:15) ..... – .....

Friday, 16 May 1997
St Helens v London Broncos (7:30 BSkyB) ..... – .....

Saturday, 17 May 1997
Paris St Germain v Sheffield Eagles (8:00) ..... – .....

Sunday, 18 May 1997
Castleford Tigers v Salford Reds (3:30) ..... – .....
Halifax Blue Sox v Wigan Warriors (3:00) ..... – .....
Oldham Bears v Leeds Rhinos (3:00) ..... – .....
Warrington Wolves v Bradford Bulls (6:35 BSkyB) ..... – .....

Thursday, 22 May 1997
Salford Reds v St Helens (7:30 BSkyB) ..... – .....

Friday, 23 May 1997
Bradford Bulls v Oldham Bears (7:30) ..... – .....
London Broncos v Warrington Wolves (7:30 BSkyB) ..... – .....
Sheffield Eagles v Halifax Blue Sox (7:30) ..... – .....
Wigan Warriors v Castleford Tigers (7:30) ..... – .....

Monday, 26 May 1997 (Bank Holiday Monday)
Castleford Tigers v Leeds Rhinos (3:30) ..... – .....
Oldham Bears v Salford Reds (3:00) ..... – .....
Paris St Germain v London Broncos (8:00) ..... – .....
St Helens v Wigan Warriors (7:30 BSkyB) ..... – .....
Warrington Wolves v Sheffield Eagles (3:00) ..... – .....

Tuesday, 27 May 1997
Halifax Blue Sox v Bradford Bulls (7:35 BSkyB) ..... – .....

Friday, 30 May 1997
Leeds Rhinos v Warrington Wolves (7:30 BSkyB) ..... – .....
Wigan Warriors v Paris St Germain (7:30) ..... – .....

Sunday, 1 June 1997
Halifax Blue Sox v St Helens (6:35 BSkyB) ..... – .....
London Broncos v Sheffield Eagles (3:00) ..... – .....
Oldham Bears v Castleford Tigers (3:00) ..... – .....
Salford Reds v Bradford Bulls (3:00) ..... – .....

Saturday, 7 June 1997
World Club Championship Round 1

Saturday, 14 June 1997
World Club Championship Round 2

Saturday, 21 June 1997
World Club Championship Round 3

Sunday, 29 June 1997
Halifax Blue Sox v Paris St Germain (3:00) ..... – .....
Leeds Rhinos v Bradford Bulls (8:00) ..... – .....
London Broncos v Castleford Tigers (3:00) ..... – .....
Oldham Bears v St Helens (3:00) ..... – .....
Salford Reds v Warrington Wolves (3:00) ..... – .....
Wigan Warriors v Sheffield Eagles (3:00) ..... – .....

Wednesday, 2 July 1997
Bradford Bulls v Castleford Tigers (7:30) ..... – .....
Leeds Rhinos v Halifax Blue Sox (7:30) ..... – .....
London Broncos v Oldham Bears (7:30) ..... – .....
Paris St Germain v Salford Reds (8.00) ..... – .....
Sheffield Eagles v St Helens (7:30) ..... – .....
Wigan Warriors v Warrington Wolves (7:30) ..... – .....

Saturday, 5 July 1997
Paris St Germain v Castleford Tigers (8:00) ..... – .....

Sunday, 6 July 1997
Leeds Rhinos v Salford Reds (3:00) ..... – .....
London Broncos v Wigan Warriors (3:00) ..... – .....
Oldham Bears v Sheffield Eagles (3:00) ..... – .....
St Helens v Bradford Bulls (6:00) ..... – .....
Warrington Wolves v Halifax Blue Sox (3:00) ..... – .....

Friday, 11 July 1997
Warrington Wolves v Leeds Rhinos (7:30) ..... – .....

Saturday, 12 July 1997
Paris St Germain v Wigan Warriors (8:00) ..... – .....

Sunday, 13 July 1997
Bradford Bulls v Salford Reds (6:00) ..... – .....
Castleford Tigers v Oldham Bears (3:30) ..... – .....
Sheffield Eagles v London Broncos (3:15) ..... – .....
St. Helens v Halifax Blue Sox (6:00) ..... – .....

Saturday, 19 July 1997
World Club Championship Round 4

Saturday, 26 July 1997
World Club Championship Round 5

Saturday, 2 August 1997
World Club Championship Round 6

Saturday, 9 August 1997
Paris St Germain v Halifax Blue Sox (8:00)
  @ Narbonne

Sunday, 10 August 1997
Bradford Bulls v Leeds Rhinos (6:00) ..... – .....
Castleford Tigers v London Broncos (3:30) ..... – .....
Sheffield Eagles v Wigan Warriors (3:15) ..... – .....
St Helens v Oldham Bears (6:00) ..... – .....
Warrington Wolves v Salford Reds (3:00) ..... – .....

Friday, 15 August 1997
Leeds Rhinos v London Broncos (7:30) ..... – .....

Saturday, 16 August 1997
Paris St Germain v Warrington Wolves (8:00)
  @ Biarritz

Sunday, 17 August 1997
Castleford Tigers v St Helens (3:30) ..... – .....
Halifax Blue Sox v Oldham Bears (3:00) ..... – .....
Sheffield Eagles v Bradford Bulls (3:15) ..... – .....
Wigan Warriors v Salford Reds (3:00) ..... – .....

Friday, 22 August 1997
Bradford Bulls v Paris St Germain (7:30) ..... – .....
Halifax Blue Sox v Castleford Tigers (7:30) ..... – .....
Leeds Rhinos v Sheffield Eagles (7:30) ..... – .....
Oldham Bears v Wigan Warriors (7:30) ..... – .....
Salford Reds v London Broncos (7:30) ..... – .....
Warrington Wolves v St Helens (7:30) ..... – .....

Monday, 25 August 1997 (Bank Holiday Monday)
Bradford Bulls v Wigan Warriors (6:00) ..... – .....
London Broncos v Halifax Blue Sox (3:00) ..... – .....
Paris St Germain v Oldham Bears (3:00) ..... – .....
Sheffield Eagles v Salford Reds (3:15) ..... – .....
St Helens v Leeds Rhinos (3:00) ..... – .....
Warrington Wolves v Castleford Tigers (3:00) ..... – .....

Sunday, 31 August 1997
Castleford Tigers v Sheffield Eagles (3:30) ..... – .....
London Broncos v Bradford Bulls (3:00) ..... – .....
Oldham Bears v Warrington Wolves (3:00) ..... – .....
Salford Reds v Halifax Blue Sox (3:00) ..... – .....
St Helens v Paris St Germain (3:00) ..... – .....
Wigan Warriors v Leeds Rhinos (3:00) ..... – .....

WORLD CLUB CHAMPIONSHIP

Chart the progress of the global powers of Rugby League, so that at the end of the season you will have a record of the inaugural World Club Championship. Space has been provided for you to fill in the teams and the scores for each match, as well as the point scorers for the Final itself.

World Club Championship: pool games

	Pool A Europe		Pool A Australasia		Pool B Europe		Pool B Australasia	
Round 1 7 June	Bradford Bulls v Penrith Panthers	.... –	Brisbane Broncos v London Broncos	.... –	Castleford Tigers v Western Reds	.... –	Adelaide Rams v Salford Reds	.... – ....
	St Helens v Auckland Warriors	.... –	Canberra Raiders v Halifax Blue Sox	.... –	Paris St Germain v Hunter Mariners	.... –	N. Queensland Cowboys v Leeds Rhinos	.... – ....
	Warrington Wolves v Cronulla Sharks	.... –	Canterbury Bulldogs v Wigan Warriors	.... –				
Round 2 14 June	Bradford Bulls v Auckland Warriors	.... –	Brisbane Broncos v Wigan Warriors	.... –	Castleford Tigers v Hunter Mariners	.... –	Adelaide Rams v Leeds Rhinos	.... – ....
	St Helens v Cronulla Sharks	.... –	Canberra Raiders v London Broncos	.... –	Sheffield Eagles v Western Reds	.... –	N. Queensland Cowboys v Oldham Bears	.... – ....
	Warrington Wolves v Penrith Panthers	.... –	Canterbury Bulldogs v Halifax Blue Sox	.... –				
Round 3 21 June	Bradford Bulls v Cronulla Sharks	.... –	Brisbane Broncos v Halifax Blue Sox	.... –	Paris St Germain v Western Reds	.... –	Adelaide Rams v Oldham Bears	.... – ....
	St Helens v Penrith Panthers	.... –	Canberra Raiders v Wigan Warriors	.... –	Sheffield Eagles v Hunter Mariners	.... –	N. Queensland Cowboys v Salford Reds	.... – ....
	Warrington Wolves v Auckland Warriors	.... –	Canterbury Bulldogs v London Broncos	.... –				
Round 4 19 July	Halifax Blue Sox v Canterbury Bulldogs	.... –	Auckland Warriors v Bradford Bulls	.... –	Leeds Rhinos v Adelaide Rams	.... –	Hunter Mariners v Castleford Tigers	.... – ....
	London Broncos v Canberra Raiders	.... –	Cronulla Sharks v St Helens	.... –	Oldham Bears v N. Queensland Cowboys	.... –	Western Reds v Sheffield Eagles	.... – ....
	Wigan Warriors v Brisbane Broncos	.... –	Penrith Panthers v Warrington Wolves	.... –				
Round 5 26 July	Halifax Blue Sox v Canberra Raiders	.... –	Auckland Warriors v St Helens	.... –	Oldham Bears v Adelaide Rams	.... –	Hunter Mariners v Paris St Germain	.... – ....
	London Broncos v Brisbane Broncos	.... –	Cronulla Sharks v Warrington Wolves	.... –	Salford Reds v N. Queensland Cowboys	.... –	Western Reds v Castleford Tigers	.... – ....
	Wigan Warriors v Canterbury Bulldogs	.... –	Penrith Panthers v Bradford Bulls	.... –				
Round 6 2 August	Halifax Blue Sox v Brisbane Broncos	.... –	Auckland Warriors v Warrington Wolves	.... –	Leeds Rhinos v N. Queensland Cowboys	.... –	Hunter Mariners v Sheffield Eagles	.... – ....
	London Broncos v Canterbury Bulldogs	.... –	Cronulla Sharks v Bradford Bulls	.... –	Salford Reds v Adelaide Rams	.... –	Western Reds v Paris St Germain	.... – ....
	Wigan Warriors v Canberra Raiders	.... –	Penrith Panthers v St Helens	.... –				

World Club Championship qualifiers (13 August)

Europe

4th place in Pool A v Top Pool B

.... – ....

Winner of the above game assume 4th placed team in quarter finals

Quarter Finals (4/5 October)

Places refer to standings in World Club Championship League tables

Europe

A European Super League 1 v Australasia Super League 4

.... – ....

B European Super League 2 v Australasia Super League 3

.... – ....

Australasia

C Australasia Super League 1 v European Super League 4

.... – ....

D Australasia Super League 2 v European Super League 3

.... – ....

Semi Finals / The Hemisphere Finals (11/12 October)

1. Winner Match A v Winner Match B

.... – ....

2. Winner Match C v Winner Match D

.... – ....

The Final (18 October, Australia)

Northern Hemisphere (Winner of semi-final 1) v Southern Hemisphere (Winner of semi-final 2)

.... – ....

.... Tries: ....

.... Goals: ....

.... DG: ....

WORLD CLUB CHAMPIONSHIP

The 12 Eurppean and 10 Australasian Super League clubs will contest the World Club Championship. Based on the previous year's domestic league tables, the top 6 in both the European Super League and the Australasian Super League form Pool A; the bottom 6 in the European Super League and the bottom 4 in the Australasian Super League form Pool B.

In Pool A matches are played in 3-week blocks, home and away, in June and July/August. Within Pool A, European and Australasian teams form separate league tables based on the results of the above fixtures. The top 3 in each table qualify for the quarter finals.

In Pool B matches are also played in 3-week blocks at the same time as the matches in Pool A. European teams play two matches, home and away, the Australasian teams play 3 home, 3 away.

Within Pool B, European and Australasian teams also form separate tables. The top team in the European table plays off against the 4th placed team in Pool A in the World Club Championship qualifier. The top team in the Australasian Pool B table automatically qualifies for the quarter finals.

Sky Sports Live Fixtures 1997

Sky Sports have scheduled 24 live matches during the first three months of the 1997 Super League season. The live games will be broadcast on Friday nights and Sunday evenings at 7.00 p.m. (kick-off 7.30 p.m.) and 6.30 p.m. (kick-off 6.35 p.m.) respectively. Within the first three months of the season every club will appear live on Sky Sports at least twice, and each club will host at least one live match at their home ground.

Premiership

The Premiership will, as usual, be played at the end of the regular Stones Super League season. In the Qualifying Round the teams finishing 5th, 6th, 7th and 8th will be at home to the 12th, 11th, 10th and 9th teams, respectively. The 1st, 2nd, 3rd and 4th teams host the Quarter-Finals, against the lowest teams, in that order, and the two highest Semi-Finalists play at home. The Final is scheduled for Old Trafford.

The provisional dates are as follows:

6/7 September 1997	Qualifying Round
13/14 September 1997	Quarter-Finals
20/21 September 1997	Semi-Finals
28 September 1997	Premiership Final

COMING AT YOU LIVE ... Super League, including Martin Crompton (left) and his Oldham Bears, will be live on Sky

Picture Credits

Allsport UK Ltd. 23/Clive Brunskill 5t; Graham Chadwick 81; Phil Cole 24, 48; Stu Forster 19, 68, 83, 107; Clive Mason 9, 16, 17, 64, 65; Ross Kinnaird 18, 71; Gary M.Prior 54; Ben Radford 29, 57; Dave Rogers 84, 89; Mark Thompson 49, 55, 56, 75, 86; Anton Want 52
Jay Town 93-103
© **Sky Sports**/Shaun Botterill 15, 46, 58, 70; Graham Chadwick 35; Mike Hewitt 14; Dave Rogers 13, 30, 36; Gerald Sunderland 7; Sam Teare 4, 12, 24, 34, 41, 42, 43, 60, 67, 85
Varley Wilkinson 5, 8, 10, 11, 20, 21, 22, 26, 27, 28, 33, 37, 38, 39, 40, 44, 45, 47, 50, 51, 53, 59, 61, 62, 63, 66, 69, 72, 73, 74, 76, 77, 79, 80, 82, 87, 88, 90, 91, 104, 106, 109, 112
Dave Williams/Photogenic 78